# Family, Friends
# and Fans

# Family, Friends and Fans

## Jason Aldean
*with* Tom Carter

Printed in the United States of America

Hardcover ISBN: 978-0-692-94151-5
Ebook ISBN: 978-0-692-94152-2

Front cover photo courtesy of Jim Wright

Back cover photo courtesy of Jimmy Cannon Photography

Cover and page design by Holly Jones

# Contents

# Preface

I'm thankful that so many people like my music. So I wrote this book to let people know a little more about the man who makes it—me.

There's an old mathematical rule that says the whole is equal to the sum of its parts. I figured that if fans saw the parts, places and people I'm made of, they'd get a better idea of who I am. And then they might enjoy my music even more.

Now, I'm obviously a singer, but I'm also the result of the many men and women from "The Big Three": my family, my friends and my fans.

This book features an array of those folks, and their positive influence on me. Over time, their words and deeds have become lessons that I carry with me today.

Some of these people I met as a child and they are still a part of my life. Others I've met more recently. Hopefully, they too will be with me forever.

Throughout this book, you'll encounter stimulating things that people have said. Others have done wonderful things that have spoken louder than words.

Benjamin Franklin said, "Experience is the best teacher, but a fool will learn from no other." I agree. But I'd expand that old saying and say that "Experience is the best teacher when you also learn from other people's experiences." Don't get me wrong. I think everyone should learn from his or her own life's ordeals. But people who don't learn from others' lives are cheating themselves.

When you learn from your own situations, you learn from one teacher. When you learn from others, you learn from a multitude.

I've titled this book "Family, Friends and Fans." It's an abbreviated diary of what I've experienced and learned over most of four decades. I hope this work is entertaining as well as uplifting, and I hope you find things that make you glad you read it.

Maybe you'll take a lesson or two for your own life, and how you chose to live it. Maybe you'll choose to live it better and better with each passing day.

# Acknowledgments

I give unlimited appreciation to Benny Brown, founder and president of Broken Bow Records (BBR). He signed me to BBR after I auditioned for Nashville's countless record companies from 1998 until 2004. The word "rejection" became a big part of my vocabulary. Were it not for Benny, you never would have heard any of my songs on the radio, television, via online media or in live performances.

"Appreciation" is an understatement regarding my timeless gratitude for Barry Williams, my father, and Debbie Wood, my mother.

My dad showed me how to make guitar chords when my hands were too small to fully grasp the neck. He consistently encouraged me throughout my childhood. When I was in high school and for a while after I graduated, my dad scheduled engagements for my band and me. He drove me to and from virtually every date. He was the first person to take me to Nashville.

My mother put up with my constant singing in the house and in the car when I was a kid. When I was 14, I wanted desperately to sing in public. My mother actually arranged for me to sing two songs at a VFW Hall with a band whose members I didn't know. Those seven minutes of performing drove my desire to one day sing for an unlimited fan base and for unlimited time. Only about ten people saw me at the VFW. But last year, nearly two million people saw me at NBA arenas, Major League Baseball parks and NFL stadiums. My mom was the beginning of all of that.

I can't thank or love enough my daughters, Kendyl and Keeley. Their dad earns his living traveling 150 days a year. When opportunity allows, the girls are with me wherever I'm performing. But whenever I'm breathing, they're in my heart.

I've loved my sister, Kasi Morstad, for every day of her life. She met with my co-writer to provide input for this book. Then, two weeks later, she sent a list of additional recollections. Her thoroughness is characteristic, and I used almost everything she said for her chapter in these pages.

I give heartfelt thanks to Vivian Williams, my stepmother, who came into my dad's life when he was a career Air Force man with a three-year-old boy. As an only child, I learned the value of family love from Vivian, her five sisters and parents. Meals at their houses were festivities laced with love and incredible food.

I applaud my record producer Michael Knox.

"Trust me," he kept saying. "I'll get us there. Trust me." I did and he did. We have seven albums and twenty-eight singles to prove it.

Brittany Layne Williams became my wife on March 21, 2015, after a high-profile courtship. I can't thank her enough for staying with me during all of that, and for vowing to stay with me forever. She's a vital part of my morale when I'm traveling, and at home. I don't know how I'd ever live without her, and I don't ever want to find out. When interviewed for this book, she was candid in answering every question she was asked.

Billy Morstad has been my friend since we were in seventh grade together. For this book, he shared painful memories of a tragedy that shaped eternal lessons for him and for me. After an emotionally draining interview, he offered to provide even more information if it were needed. And he meant it.

Tully Kennedy, Rich Redmond, Kurt Allison, Jay Jackson, and Jack Sizemore are the core of my instrumental sound. They ride in a tour bus from venue to venue year in and year out. Sometimes, the miles are grinding, but their music is always electrifying.

Kevin Neal is an executive at William Morris Endeavor (WME), the largest talent booking and artist management company in the nation. He was my first agent at another agency. When he moved to WME, I moved with him. He gets me a mountain of concert dates that keep me in front of my fans. He has shared in these pages a few of our career experiences that years ago led to some of my most valuable lessons learned.

Tommy Powell gave me a job delivering Pepsi and other soft drinks while I was in high school. That may not sound out of the ordinary, and it wasn't. But Tommy's work ethic expanded my own. Back in the day, he often drove my band's van to our shows throughout the Southeast. Wanting to help my career, Tommy paid for his own meals and lodging, and was never paid a cent.

Justin Weaver showed the power of persistence and he has kindly shared his story in this book.

Remember Compact Discs? Angela Pitts used to sell my CD at shows. She also rode in the van with my first band and me from date to date. For this book, Angela has brought fascinating and constructive memories from the years she volunteered with me in my career's formative days.

While I've done my best to put words together for this book, words fail when I try to thank my fans. More than anything, my fan base has been the bedrock of my career. This book is not just a small token of my appreciation to the fans; I hope it's also a worthy tribute to them.

Like my music, this book would not have transpired had it not been for my loyal and energetic fans.

My first book is dedicated to them.

—Jason Aldean

My heartfelt gratitude goes to Janie Carter, my assistant for twenty-seven years; my wife for fifteen. She's been my production staple for all but one of the nineteen books I've written. In addition, she's my source of consolation and inspiration when I get writer's block, and my well of determination goes dry.

Additionally, I would like to thank Sherry Jolly, Holly Jones, Mary Lawson, David Shannon and Jessica Smith.

I'm a senior citizen. Until almost twelve years ago, I was an illegal drug user. I've been completely free of illegal drugs since February 24, 2006.

Recently, I met Jason Aldean who doesn't believe in age discrimination. He also believes that anyone who breaks a destructive habit should not be penalized for his past, or restrained in his future.

So he and I wrote this book.

America's senior citizens age 65 and over will total approximately 50 million in 2017, according to the U.S. Census Bureau. An estimated 24.6 million Americans aged 12 and older are illicit drug users, according to Samhsa.gov. They should know they have a non-judgmental, solid friend in Jason. His first priority is to issue second chances.

Thank you, Jason, thank you.

—Tom Carter

# 1

# Beginnings

I've always been somewhat of a loner, even in front of 50,000 people or on coast-to-coast television. I was equally alone inside a school classroom where I wanted to learn only one thing.

"What time will class end?"

My interests weren't in textbooks. I didn't care about their contents. Why should I? I didn't know who wrote them!

If you think that sounds outrageous, it's not when compared to many other experiences in my youth and childhood. Experience, I stress, really is the best teacher. And many things I've been taught have led to permanent conclusions.

My first lesson was that love begins whenever and wherever it wants.

I hadn't been born the day my dad, Barry Williams, then 17, was walking though the Pendleton Homes public housing complex in South Macon, Georgia, where he encountered the former Debbie Wooten, 15, my eventual mother. Dad had found Mom and her mother, Annie Mae Wooten, stalled in a station wagon. It was attached by a rope to an old car trying to pull it.

Trying to impress my mother, Dad offered to steer the junker while Annie Mae drove the lead car.

Neither woman told Dad that the pull car had no brake lights. Each time Annie Mae hit her brakes, my dad slammed into the rear of the pull car!

When that two-car motorcade reached the repair shop, both vehicles needed work! I guess you could say my future parents' very first outing was filled with collisions.

As was their future, it turned out. My mom and dad divorced when I was three, but they've remained friends to this day, 37 years after parting.

When I was four, my father met the former Vivian Melo, a Cuban who eventually became my stepmother. She was one of six sisters who showed me that love flourishes even more among large numbers.

Vivian's large family introduced me to a new culture laced with noisy happiness. My Cuban grandparents, Abuela and Abuelo Melo, were hosts to loud family gatherings, affectionate chaos among two parents, six sisters, their husbands and all of their children!

They were like the Walton Family on too much caffeine!

Everyone seemingly talked louder than everyone else. As a pre-schooler, I sometimes thought they were arguing, and on the brink of brawling! Not true. They were just a fun family whose members were much noisier than the silence at my mom's.

To this day, I can hear the Cubans' carryings-on, and smell the aromas of roasted pork, black beans and rice and fried plantains filling Abuela's kitchen.

Those people were hard-working and obeyed the law—their own.

Abuelo kept 30 illegal fighting roosters inside a backyard pen.

I wondered why the police didn't see and hear those crowing birds? Why didn't lawmen notice there were no hens and no eggs? Clearly, that pen was a dirt and wire training camp whose feathered soldiers fought to the death.

How did Abuelo get away with that?

On weekends, he'd put two fighting roosters inside a burlap sack, and hand-carry them to organized fights. In each skirmish, one of his roosters, or its opponent, bled to death from razors attached to both birds' feet.

Those fights were blood baths that would make today's animal rights activists cringe. But I knew nothing about the rights of animals when I was that small.

I always knew when one of Abuelo's roosters was killed. We ate it that night for dinner!

Inside the free-spirited Melo family, I also met Papo, a step-cousin who was two years older than I was. He was foul-mouthed and taught me how to cuss. He was a hard-fisted fighter and took no guff from anyone. It seemed natural that everyone assumed he'd someday live outside the law and behind bars.

Instead, to our surprise, he became a deputy sheriff and holds that job to this day! I wonder if he arrests owners of fighting roosters?

When Dad, Mom and I were at home, I fell in love with another kind of sound. Music. Sometimes it was loud, but it always had purpose. Enjoyment.

About that same time, I found audio companionship in cassette tapes. Each song yielded the singer's feelings, and I could always find a song with feelings that matched my own.

I was an only child but I was never entirely alone. Music was my playmate. So what if I couldn't speak to it?

It spoke to me.

My dad showed me how to handle the tapes and how to take special care with vinyl records. I carefully held the vinyl so as not to rub its surface. Dad had shown me how such rubbing scratched the music.

Those delicate tapes and records became miniature trophies in my small hands.

Recordings were great, but live music had its own excitement. One of the first emotional rushes I ever felt was from hearing Dad and his brothers, Uncle Ray and Uncle Roy "perform." I was blown away by their bloodline harmonies, and the way they coaxed rhythm from chords played on their guitars.

I yearned to do that.

So Dad drew six horizontal lines on paper. Each represented a guitar string. There, he drew large dots that represented my fingers and where they should go among vertical lines. Those lines represented guitar frets.

I used that diagram to place my real fingers on a real guitar neck. I practiced that position daily while Dad was at work.

Dad taught me two more chords using the same system. In maybe a week, I learned a three-chord pattern that allowed me to accompany myself on guitar as I sang.

My first rendition was "The Cowboy Rides Away" by George Strait.

I didn't realize it at the time, but it was my persistence that had paid off—my determination was more vital than any "talent" I might have possessed at that young age.

Now, while I do understand there is awesome value in talent and new ideas, I've foremostly learned the lesson that nothing is as productive as persistence. Nothing.

Later in these pages, I'll talk about my persistence in staying the course when pursuing a music recording deal. Then, as now, hundreds of singers in Nashville wanted the same thing.

They just didn't want it as long as I.

That same brand of drive intensified when I was thirteen or fourteen years old, and Dad bought me my first guitar, a cheap Bentley whose strings were too high off the neck, and wouldn't stay in tune. I actually had to tune that guitar after every song.

Dad told me, "If you learn to play this Bentley, I'll buy you a better guitar."

Those words may stand as the most valuable proposition ever spoken to me in my entire life!

Today, that old Bentley and my second guitar hang on the wall in my "Man Cave," that place where I process the future by recalling the past, among other things.

Recalling my childhood, I lived most of the time with my mom, a civil servant who's now retired from the National Park Service. She transferred a lot of times with her government job. That meant another apartment, another public school and another group of unfamiliar kids. I'd attended eight schools by the time I'd entered eighth grade.

People ask if I hated leaving old friends so frequently. I didn't see it that way. Instead, I saw each move as an opportunity to create new friends.

I feel that same way to this day. I love surprises rooted in suspense. What's more suspenseful than meeting people you don't know so you can do things you never have? I often regretted leaving old friends, but never dreaded making new ones.

By the time I was 5, I was playing organized sports and I loved it. In grade school, I was an athlete, and excelled in baseball.

When Mom was at work, I spent too much time alone. The silence was deafening to an only child filled with energy that couldn't be released by playing with a brother or sister.

So I was always eager to meet new kids. And I mastered the art of doing it. It evolved into a lesson that I practice to this day.

Simply put, show new people you can do something that pleases them. When I was young, it was sports. Now, it's music, and my obsession to perform songs that entertain my audiences.

Back before kindergarten, music began to evolve as my driving force, almost equal to sports. I sang a lot on 12-hour drives from my mother's house in Macon, Georgia, to my dad's in Homestead, Florida.

Alabama was my favorite band in the early 1980s. My dad let me play their cassette tapes. I completely wore out some of them.

Soon thereafter, music grew from a pastime into a passion.

On those long and dreary drives, it became a companion made of melodies and rhythms. When the hour was late and the journey was long, I was touched by the heartfelt lyrics of those country ballads. Alone in a car's dark and sprawling back seat, I felt the moods of the writers who wrote those songs about real feelings in real lives like mine.

It was like someone told my secrets in songs, and Alabama's lead singer, Randy Owen, was singing directly to me, or so it seemed.

Music is entertainment, of course. But it's also a "friend" that can fit with any mood at any time. How many *people* can be trusted to do that?

I learned that lesson in my makeshift classroom, that four-door sedan cruising the monotony of the miles from one household to another.

My emotional attachment to music persists to this day.

And whenever I start missing something from my past, I can always play or perform a song that comforts me in the present. The tune might be happy, sad, upbeat, slow or thoughtful. No matter.

Music became one of my life's priorities—a priority I never changed and never will.

# Vivian

In 1979, when I was two years old, a young woman named Vivian and her mother, Rosa Melo, happened to see me in a Florida grocery store. Vivian didn't know me, nor did she see my dad's face, as his back was turned to her.

Without speaking, Vivian, Rosa, my dad and I left the store in different directions. Even if we'd spoken, we wouldn't have expected to see each other again.

Two years later, my dad coincidentally began dating Vivian. He told her he had a son. She saw my picture and recognized me from having seen me only once 24 months earlier in that grocery store!

Rosa told Vivian, "That proves your relationship with that man is meant to be." And it was.

Vivian Williams has been my stepmother for 35 years. During that time, I've learned much of Vivian's life story,

including her struggle to flee to America during Prime Minister
Fidel Castro's Cuban régime. Vivian, her parents and five sisters
fought continuously from 1965 until their staggered departures
from Cuba in 1970.

Egidio Melo, Vivian's father, had been outspoken in Cuba
about his hate for Castro's suppression of human rights. As a
result, soldiers came to Vivian's house to seize her dad's guns.
The government also took his job as a welder, and moved him
away into something resembling a concentration camp.

Cuban soldiers had hidden beside Vivian's modest home
in the wee hours. There, they overheard Egidio talking about
breaking rules inside Castro's régime. Suddenly, the soldiers
broke down the family's doors, and took their father at gunpoint
to a concentration camp.

Vivian and her family, including five sisters, were allowed to
see Egidio about every two months. Vivian continued to go to
school. To earn a meager living, her older sister knitted sweaters,
and her mother took in laundry. During summers, when school
was out, 13-year-old Vivian and some of her sisters were taken
by bus to harvest vegetables and fruit from the government's
fields and orchards. At night, the girls lived in barracks.

Through persistence and repeated filing of paperwork,
Vivian, her mother and four sisters were eventually allowed to
leave the country. The fifth sister was allowed to depart two
months later in 1970.

Vivian and her entire family went to upstate New York
where they had a relative. They later moved to Puerto Rico and
ultimately landed in Florida.

In time, Vivian entered a marriage that lasted only seven months. She became a housekeeper at a hospital's intensive care unit. There, she mopped floors and cleaned toilets. Eventually, she landed a job at a telephone company.

Vivian had a friend at work who happened to hire my dad to repair wallpaper. While my dad was working, the friend had Vivian come over to visit, thereby secretly arranging a blind date between Vivian and Dad.

Of course, neither knew that the meeting was going to happen and the union was quickly put at risk when the friend told Dad that Vivian hadn't had a date in four years.

"Something is wrong with her," he said.

He didn't call Vivian for four days after meeting her. At that point, she thought he never would.

But he did call, and their first date was like a television comedy. The two went to a Chinese restaurant where Vivian's vocabulary was mostly Cuban. The waitress spoke mostly Chinese. Dad spoke English. The meal ended quickly.

Perhaps still hungry, Dad and Vivian left the restaurant to see "The Night the Lights Went Out in Georgia," a 1981 movie about a struggling country singer. Vivian thought the movie was sad. She bawled through most of the film, clung to my dad who she barely knew, and spotted his sleeve with tears and make-up.

I wonder how sad she'd have been if she'd totally understood the dialogue?

At the time, Dad lived in Homestead, Florida, where he was stationed in the Air Force. Vivian wanted the relationship to work. She hoped Dad would marry her, but, she has recently revealed, he lacked the courage to ask.

A lot of women would have taken off. But Vivian was as wise as she was independent. Even though Dad had a male roommate, Vivian asked if she could move in with them. Dad said yes.

He became her lover; the roommate became her "brother." Everyone was happy.

"I told him we could live together for a while to get to know each other," she said. "I didn't want the marriage to fail."

It didn't and still hasn't. After a year, Dad proposed. Eventually, they had a daughter, Kasi, seven years younger than I.

When I was a growing boy, Vivian regularly took Kasi and me to the Florida beach along the Atlantic ocean. She bought me my first piñata. She and my dad took me to the loud and happy homes of her sisters, parents and children. She once had to search through the night for me when I sneaked out to crash a birthday party with some girls. She always came to shows that Dad booked when I was a teenager. And she comes to some of my arena shows to this day.

While I was still in high school, Vivian listened to me for hours as I tried to decide whether to chase a career in baseball or in music.

Through it all, she taught me something that she might not have realized.

An old saying claims, "The hard times that you go through build character, making you a much stronger person."

Vivian taught me that hardship can also manufacture love. I adopted that statement as a lesson learned from Vivian.

In 1998, when I officially moved away from Vivian and my dad, I repeatedly faced the rejections of Nashville's music industry big shots. I'll talk more about that in following pages. To put it mildly, I underwent a seven-year, uphill battle filled with setbacks.

Back then, some days I withstood the fight for my musical career by remembering Vivian's experience. When she was my age, she was fighting poverty and life-threatening political oppression. Later, she faced a language barrier and lousy jobs.

Unlike me, she didn't get to fight for a career. She fought mostly for any job she could get, and a better way to live.

In those Castro years, she almost fought for life itself.

She survived all of it. With Dad and me, she triumphed.

I mentioned at the beginning of this book that I'm thankful for my permanent lessons. Most are drawn from my own experiences. But some are drawn from the lives of the most influential people in my life. Vivian is among them.

In life, I've learned that when you want something more than anything else, look to others who fought without ceasing for the fulfillment of their dreams.

Occasionally, you might look toward Vivian.

The bases were loaded with two men out in the bottom of the ninth inning. The count was three balls and two strikes.

The pitcher could have thrown a curve ball or a sinker.

Instead, the hurler slung a fastball, the only pitch the pitcher knew.

The batter pulled back, swung with all of his might, and completely missed the toss speeding down the middle.

"Strike three!" the umpire yelled, "you're out! Game over!"

The winning bench was emptied by joyful players who met the pitcher halfway between the dugout and the mound.

In their celebration, I hoped they wouldn't hurt her.

That's right. "Her."

The former Kasi Williams was a thirteen-year-old girl playing regulation baseball against all-boy teams. Kasi could fan most of those batters with ease.

She was special for another reason. She was my little sister. The daintiest player in her entire league, seven years younger than I, could routinely pitch, hit and run against boys older than she. To me, she was always the Most Valuable Player in all of her baseball games. Today, she remains one of my Most Valuable Players in the game of life. Currently, she thrives as a pharmaceutical salesperson, wife and mother of three.

Soon, she'll join many of my family members to live near me on property I bought just outside of Nashville.

Although she hasn't played in years, Kasi still credits some of her baseball skills to those learned in her childhood backyard. There, I became her very first unofficial coach. I'd often ask her to pitch to me while I showed her how to confuse a batter. She wanted me to pitch to her, but I was bigger and stronger, and didn't want to hurt her.

"If you don't let me bat a while I'm going to go into the house," she sometimes said when she was in grade school.

So I'd throw her my most gentle pitch. She'd complain that I was throwing like a girl.

Then we played some more, a brother and sister in the summertime sun passing the time in harmless ways we thought would never end. And they never will, at least not in Kasi's and my memories.

I remember when she entered junior high school. There, she was sought by a coach to play baseball against boys. But Kasi's tomboy days were behind her, and she opted to play softball. I was happy about the transition, but a little bit taken aback, as my rough and tumble sister and backyard companion would soon be wearing lipstick and pursuing boys.

Baseball wouldn't be her motivation.

I thought back even farther to the days when Kasi was four and played "T-Ball." I showed her how to swing a bat to knock a ball off a pedestal. Each time she hit the Wiffle ball, she was filled with excitement as if she'd hit a grand slam in the World Series.

But her T-Ball excitement wasn't restrained to the playing field.

I fondly recall days when I moved the furniture inside our living room to construct a makeshift baseball diamond. I used a pillow for home base. I'd throw a tennis ball against the wall, and let Kasi run the bases, while I did the play-by-play announcing.

My petite sister would sometimes slide into home base while I tagged her at the plate. She'd insist she was safe, and I usually agreed.

That went on for hours until one of our parents was expected to arrive. Kasi and I then moved all of the furnishings back to their proper places, and no one ever knew that a big brother-little sister pennant race had been played on a "regulation field" called our family living room.

I remember watching her grow from a playful kindergarten student to a feisty little girl. A few years later, older girls wanted to be around Kasi, who was still in childhood.

"They're just hanging out around me so they can get close to you," Kasi often said.

I recall Kasi tagging along soon after I'd gotten my driver's license. She and I rode around town while blasting Guns N' Roses or Clay Walker or Tracy Lawrence on the car's sound system.

I have scores of memories that would mean nothing to anyone except Kasi and me, including our hours at the beach where we were "body surfers" or "Boogie Boarders."

Meanwhile, Kasi's mother—my stepmother—Vivian, read a book while seemingly watching our every move. How did she do that?

Kasi sometimes came to my Young Guns shows long before she was legally allowed in bars. From the bandstand, I saw guys flirting with her. Knowing I had fire in my eyes, I glared right at them. The guys quickly interpreted my hostility. She would get mad about it.

When Kasi was a student at the University of Georgia, the first time I visited, she and I went to a football game. (The Georgia Bulldogs are my favorite team!)

Afterwards, we decided to have a few drinks. That was one of the first times I realized my little sister could legally drink alcohol. She insisted on leading the way as she and I headed to a bar together for the first time.

The two of us walked for miles.

But the clubs were only minutes away. We could have taken the shorter route if Kasi had admitted she had no idea where she was leading me.

I remember how I appreciated Kasi's pride the first time I performed at the University of Georgia. She and her friends were there, cheering me on at one of the most special engagements of my career.

I'd earlier played Nashville's Wild Horse Saloon, the last of my showcases intended to land a recording deal. Kasi knew that if I failed to get a deal, I'd move back to Georgia the next day after seven years of struggling in Nashville.

That night, to give me moral support, my dad hired limousines for Kasi and her friends. They rode from Athens to Nashville and back in one night. As a result, Kasi had been there when I was offered a recording contract, the biggest break in my career at that time.

I could continue recalling wonderful times between my little sister and me.

There are life lessons in almost all of my nostalgia. For example, an old saying goes, "Familiarity breeds contempt." In others words, people who spend too much time together see their fondness evaporate.

I've learned that cliché is wrong. My sister will always be seven years younger than me. But just as we grew up together, we'll grow old together.

Our brother/sister love will always change—for the better.

I'll always be there to advise her, sometimes when she wants, and sometimes when she doesn't. I'll do it with the sincerity I once gave to a four-year-old child.

Maybe I can help her with advice on how to raise children with all of the really important things, such as getting good grades in school, respecting their country, obeying their parents and . . . how to build a living room baseball field with a pillow for home plate.

# 4

# Billy

Billy Morstad entered my life in the eighth grade at Windsor Academy in Macon, Georgia, twenty-fiveyears ago. I was surprised to learn he recently admitted to someone that he hadn't liked me at first, but he and I bonded during baseball season. He played third base, and I shoveled many of his throws out of the dirt while playing first base.

"Jason pulled so many of my throws off the ground that my dad nicknamed him 'Scoop'," Billy said. I've never had a biological brother, but if I had, I doubt he would have been any closer to me than Billy.

"As far as I can remember, we didn't do anything without the other throughout high school," Billy recalled in a December 2015 interview.

Our paths took different directions when Billy accepted a baseball scholarship to Middle Georgia College in Cochran,

Georgia. I focused on my music. Although we went separate ways, we were never apart, not mentally, emotionally or loyally.

Today, he's my brother-in-law, and he and I are partners in a business unrelated to sports or music. During our quarter century as friends, I have absorbed a solid lesson from my relationship with Billy: True new friends might stand beside you if you ask. But true old friends will stand beside you whether you ask or not.

Also, newer friends will feel sorry about your pain. A seasoned friend will actually feel it, even the smallest pain. Any true friend, new or old, is a priceless thing to have. And long-term friendships thrive even when friends develop different interests.

Billy didn't set out to teach all of that to me. But over time, he made me realize a big part of it.

He didn't play baseball during his final season at Middle Georgia. At age 22, he and his wife, Melissa, had a daughter with another on the way.

"When she (the second daughter) arrived, it just became time to hang up the cleats and get serious about life," he said. "Baseball just wasn't fun anymore."

For Billy and Melissa, life in general soon wasn't fun either. She developed a cyst on her breast, and experts drained it. Six months later, the cyst became inflamed and was surgically removed. A biopsy diagnosed cancer. She underwent a mastectomy of her right breast and one of her lymph nodes was removed.

"Supposedly, the margins were all clean and she completed her chemotherapy and was just about done with it," Billy recalled. "I think she had eight to ten radiation treatments left. She had things going on, and we went back and requested a CT scan and an MRI. They found out that basically cancer had spread all over her body at that point."

In all, Melissa underwent 18 rounds of chemotherapy and 33 radiation treatments. Ultimately, tumors were found on her brain and elsewhere in her body. Soon afterwards, Melissa arrived for her final chemotherapy treatment, but doctors saw no reason to administer it. Her blood levels were immensely high. Physicians said there was nothing else they could do.

Melissa died two and a half weeks later. She left Billy and his daughters, ages four and five. Approximately 300 people attended Melissa's funeral. Following the service, Billy disappeared without visiting with anyone.

"I didn't want to stand in the line to hear everybody say how sorry they were for my loss," he said.

I totally understood. Billy probably didn't want person after person telling him to call if he needed anything. Words like that at a time like that may be polite, but they're often ineffective. He didn't need a thing from anyone nearly as much as he needed Melissa.

Billy had something else to face. Immediately following the funeral, he knew he had to return to his home where his daughters would soon arrive. Totally confused, the girls asked why their mother wasn't in her bed.

"I basically said, 'Your mother is now in Heaven helping other people with cancer so maybe they don't get sick or maybe they don't lose their hair.' They took those words, and embraced them and drew pictures of Melissa as an angel."

Billy had lived all of his life as an outgoing and likable guy. Two months after the funeral, he was deep into depression. Despite their mother's new home in Heaven, his daughters saw their dad crying. I don't know how he explained that. Billy fell into what he called a "pity party" for two months. My best friend was emotionally down to a depth I'd never seen, in him, or in anyone else. I totally understood it, though. Who wouldn't? If our friendship is based on anything, it's based on truth. And truth sometimes must be told despite the circumstances.

So I told Billy what I thought, and to stop his self-described "pity party." I said it was time to stop dwelling on himself, or even Melissa. I reminded him he had two little girls, and it was time to focus on them.

All of that seemed like the obvious thing that needed to be said. I wasn't going to let fear stop me, not even if I hurt Billy. His pain would have eventually stopped. His girls' need for a daddy never would. Not until I began writing this book did I realize that my directness helped usher Billy through the biggest trial he'd ever undergone. He said he was comforted because he and I did what we'd always done. We talked with bare-bones honesty.

In time, Billy grew stronger as a widower. I became a better man because I had a friend in Billy, someone who wanted the truth, despite his suffering. I guess you could say that Billy and I have a solid friendship based partially on words. Not necessarily the *polite* words, but the *honest* words.

If I ever believed in non-filtered dialogue, it was during and after Billy's loss of Melissa. Our directness just confirmed what I'd believed for years: that honesty is one of life's most valuable lessons, and blessings. Total truthfulness might not guarantee a totally happy life. But dishonesty guarantees an unhappy life, at least to a degree.

Billy's children eventually accepted their little family as it was; a daddy at home and a mother in Heaven. He began to do motherly things, including the buying of their clothes by picking out identical outfits in multiple colors. He even learned how to fix their hair into ponytails, despite their claims that the hairdos were too tight.

He began dating my sister, Kasi, and, at first, no one in my family knew about it. Once my dad and I understood there was a potential pairing, we remembered some rowdy things Billy and I did in high school. Instantly, I wasn't in favor of Billy becoming my brother-in-law.

Neither was my dad. But one night, Kasi stayed up all night to surprise him at 4:30 a.m., just as he was getting out of bed to go to work. While Dad was wiping sleep from his eyes, Kasi started the conversation with something like this, according to Billy:

"I think I've met the right man and I want to seriously date him," Kasi said.

"Who is it?" Dad sleepily replied.

"Billy!" she said.

"Billy who?" Dad replied.

"Billy . . . Jason's Billy!"

You mean Billy Morstad?" Dad asked.

"Yes . . . Billy Morstad!"

"HELL NO!!!" Dad said.

October 2016, marked Kasi and Billy's nine-year anniversary. That relationship is also rooted in absolute truth. Before marrying Billy, Kasi dropped a bomb on him, and said she wanted to adopt his daughters. Without the adoption, I don't think she would have married Billy.

Billy told her that decision was entirely her own. Today, including Kasi and Billy's biological daughter, my sister has one husband and three daughters. So Billy lives with four females, of whom two are teenagers, both into boys.

That situation marks the first time I have nothing to say to Billy. The fact is, I haven't got a clue.

# Helpers

I was never a kid who wanted to play with toy cars and trucks. In fact, I don't remember playing much of anything except sports, especially baseball, racquetball and football.

Each year, while living with my mother in Macon, Georgia, I wouldn't miss an Atlanta Braves games on Ted Turner's Atlanta TBS, his cable television network. I had no idea that one day I'd get a "tryout" for the Braves.

In the seventh grade, I played organized school baseball for the first time. In time, I played on other organized teams until I graduated from high school.

After each season in Macon, I'd make the All-Star team, but I never got to play in the All-Star games. Instead, I moved to Florida every year to spend my summer with Dad.

I was always eager to see him, but always regretted leaving my Georgia team. I would have disliked an entire summer in Florida without baseball.

And I never had one, thanks to my dad.

He knew that, come every spring, baseball was more than a big part of my life. It *was* my life.

So he found a Florida team that let me play all summer. That Georgia-Spring/Florida-Summer schedule stayed with me until I was 18.

And it taught me another of my life lessons that I believe to this day.

No matter how big your problem, unless it's an incurable disease, you can almost always find a solution—especially if you have an interested and trusted helper.

I had a second helper in those days—my natural mother.

After returning each fall to Macon, and putting baseball aside during the winter, I resumed enduring school and pursuing my love of music. Around age 13, I wanted to take the music a step further. I wanted to play publicly.

In those days, Mom and I were still living in a modest apartment, as she had little money, especially for recreation. She and my Aunt Betty practiced an inexpensive pastime, playing bingo at a VFW Hall attached to a small cocktail lounge.

My mother had a bingo friend who had a friend who knew the nightclub's manager. He agreed to let Mom's only son fulfill his musical fantasy by playing at the VFW Hall.

For the first time, I sang publicly for people, most of whom I didn't know. I do that to this day.

At the VFW Hall, I made history, if only to myself. And I made a breakthrough, also if only to myself.

I proved that I really could do something that I'd fantasized for months.

To some folks, my dream of playing the VFW might've seemed small, but so what? I made it come true.

That tiny bar was out-of-the way. No limousines were parked outside. There were no lines to enter, and no dress code to obey. There wasn't a marquee, only an electric sign saying "Two-for-One Bingo."

It's safe to say the press ignored the little place and my two-song sit-in. I was also somewhat ignored by ten sleepy customers inside the dimly lit and otherwise silent bar. Maybe they withheld applause so they wouldn't awaken each other.

I debuted with John Anderson's "Seminole Wind" and finished with Merle Haggard's "Silver Wings." I didn't expect an encore. That's good. I didn't get one.

Remember, the crowd was small enough to fit inside a large van. No matter. I owe each of those people.

Those two songs I sang were the most significant part of my musical life to that point. Everyone starts somewhere. I didn't consider those songs as a career launch. I didn't consider them as anything, except my finally getting to sing publicly.

For days earlier, I'd been afraid of something I'd yearned to do. Yet I did it! I proved to myself that I not only had music in me, I also had courage.

All along, I had trusted my parents. Now, more than ever, I trusted myself. My overcoming of fear was an emotional rush back then. It still is whenever I occasionally confront fear to this day.

From that one experience at the bingo hall I learned two lessons:

- Everybody has fear, but not everyone faces it. Once they do, they become a little less fearful, and a bit more courageous. That process works time after time.

- I got that VFW job because of my mom's relationship with someone. To this day, I realize the value of relationships. People who hide from other people aren't only lonely; they also deprive themselves of opportunities in work, personal growth and overall quality of life.

I've never been a procrastinating kind of guy regarding things I really like. And I've always liked singing for people. So I began to sit in with more and more bands around Macon. After each gig, my self-confidence got a bit stronger.

I entered and won many talent contests, and earned enough money to buy my first vehicle, a 1982 Toyota pickup with a rusted out tailgate. It got me from job to job. The distances weren't any longer than they would have been if I'd ridden in a Bentley.

In those lean and fun-filled days, I sang cover tunes that were a part of radio popularity surveys. Garth Brooks, Clint Black and Alabama songs went over very well with audiences.

During those early performances, I learned a valuable lesson that is a part of my performing life to this day: Sing songs that your crowd wants to hear. They paid admission to listen to them.

That sounds like an obvious approach to performing. But I've met a lot of musicians who ignore it. Those guys have attitudes that say, "Hey man, I'm an artist. I'm going to sing only what I like and I don't care what the public wants."

I understand that. After all, today I record only songs I like. And I've learned that if I like the song, then my fondness will catch on with my audiences.

I've learned to gauge the audiences' tastes very quickly after getting on stage. Some crowds aren't instantly impressed. For those, I must work harder to give them a good time. Other crowds leap to their feet the second I step on stage. Most come to hear my hits, and that's what they get.

Back to my youth.

Four years after my VFW gig, I formed "Jason Aldean and the Young Guns," my first band. A lot of new bands have to work wherever they can get it. My band and I were fortunate, and quickly got a "sit-down gig," a place we played regularly called "Nashville South."

With the exception of our 23-year-old bass player, I was the oldest guy in the group. But I was still a minor, and I was playing in a bar I couldn't legally enter. That little infraction probably made the whole ordeal a bit more fun.

But I faced another law—nature's law—that applies to everyone . . . the need for sleep.

From Wednesday to Saturday night, I played music five hours a night until 1 a.m. With luck, I could be asleep by 2 a.m. before my alarm clock rang at 7 a.m. Then, after school, I'd practice baseball or play a game before gulping my supper to rush to the 9 p.m. show.

I was running on adrenaline. It often seems as though I'm still running that fast. I just don't get to play baseball these days. And I can legally enter a bar.

I've learned that a fascinating part of life is rooted in unpredictability. I've also learned that nothing is more unpredictable than human behavior.

Think about it:

- Your closest loved one may have broken your heart or filled you with bliss when you least expected it.

- Your child may have exhibited an abrupt display of maturity that was beyond his or her calendar years. Your heart was instantly touched, and you realized once again that having a baby was the right thing to do all along.

- You may have undergone a chance, first-time encounter with someone you assumed was a role model simply because he was twice your age. You naturally expected him to be as boring as other men his age. Instead, he became a human example of unpredictability—a walking and talking exercise in fun and surprises.

I've learned that people love unexpected behavior or attitudes that enhance their own lives.

I was ambushed with a happy surprise at age 15, one year too young to work for Pepsi Cola Co., according to its employment rules.

I'd been playing baseball most of my young life, and was singing in bars after my public debut at that VFW Hall. Now I wanted a summer job just to have some "walking around" money.

But how would I get a job? How would I work it if I found one? I didn't own a car and I didn't have a driver's license.

On a Georgia spring afternoon, I was hanging around Macon's Bloom Field Softball Park. I sometimes watched the girls play organized softball there.

Someone approached the softball coach, Tommy Powell, a Pepsi delivery truck driver, and told him I needed a job.

"I knew who Jason was and I'd also read about him and his music in the newspapers," Tommy related in 2015. "And I know what it's like to want a job but you can't get one. So I broke the rules and hired him."

For the rest of that summer and two more, I rode in a Pepsi truck where Tommy and I delivered soft drinks to bars, restaurants, dispensing machines and grocery stores. We traveled as many as 110 miles in a day to deliver thousands of canned or bottled containers we pushed with a dolly.

At age 15, I wasn't exactly in love with rules. So I may have thought it was cool when Tommy broke the hiring rules at Pepsi, a big company with lots of rules. The fact that he did that to help me, someone he casually knew, really impressed me.

Even to this day, I'm not fond of rules—especially when they prevent someone's honest need from an honest job.

So, as soon as school was out, I was off to a new life on the bottom step toward corporate success. While I didn't like or stay with corporate life, I stayed with Tommy, someone whose surprise entry into my life became a lifelong friendship.

Looking back, I realize that I was largely drawn to Tommy because of his sense of fair play. He'd do exactly what he was paid to do, and sometimes even more. He never took advantage of people. But, just as impressive to a teenage boy, Tommy wouldn't let anyone take advantage of him or me, his friend.

I try to practice those same traits to this day myself. Doing the right thing, even if it's difficult, eventually leaves you with peace of mind.

I saw that first-hand in Tommy during a rainstorm. He and and I pulled up in front of a grocery store where we unloaded two hundred cases of soft drinks. That's 4,800 cans.

The wheels on our dollies were muddy from the falling water outside. When we finished, the store proprietor was outraged because our dolly had left tracks on his concrete floor.

Tommy told the guy that he'd mop up the mess, as he always did during rainfall. No matter. The guy kept right on complaining. Then, he directed his angry words at Tommy personally. Then, he started cussing Tommy.

"Let me tell you something," Tommy said, "If you keep talking like that Jason and I will load up every one of these drinks."

"Are you kidding?" I said softly to Tommy.

We'd already unloaded the giant load. I didn't want to reload it.

No matter. The storekeeper kept swearing, so Tommy and I began reloading our cargo. We took out every can that we'd taken inside.

"'I've already done a day's work, can I go home now?'" Tommy recalled that I'd said, years later.

Not to be. Many others stops were scheduled for the rest of that same day. I may have moaned.

Pretty soon, a supervisor from the Pepsi office called Tommy. He ordered him to take back the drinks. Tommy agreed to do that, but only if the proprietor called and apologized to him. The angry store owner called and told Tommy he was sorry.

Tommy took back the entire load of all of those cans, and he and I unloaded them. Again.

"'Now can I go home?'" Tommy remembered I said.

The answer was still no.

I learned that true friends take you as all you are and are not. In Tommy's case, he took me as the no frills singer and musician that I was then and now.

With no radio in his truck, I was free to sing to Tommy all day as we rode the streets and roads in and around Macon.

"I don't need a radio in here," Tommy once said. "I've got you."

A lot of adults would have been annoyed by a teenage boy who constantly sang. But not Tommy.

Eventually, we got a truck with a portable radio that we played most all of each working day. I wonder if Tommy did that so he wouldn't have to listen to me?

If so, it backfired on him. I sang with every song on the dial. In those days, I was always aware of new song releases, and most of the famous standards.

"So there we was, going down the road from one stop to another, and Jason was singing and beating on the dashboard to keep with the rhythm," Tommy said. "It was mighty good times."

Maybe I took it for granted then, but I don't today. Really good friends not only take you as you are, they also don't try to force to you to change, especially when it comes to what you love. To a large part, I learned all of that from Tommy.

He even amended his schedule just to accommodate me. If my dad had scheduled a show for my band and me on Friday night, Tommy and I would work extra time on Mondays and sometimes other days. That way, I could get off work on Friday to travel to my show. Then, when I got there, Tommy would be in the audience.

Eventually, he would regularly drive the van to take the band and me to bookings in several nightclubs. That continued for almost three years.

This guy, who'd entered my life without warning, was then endorsing my life and lifestyle. He was never paid a cent, and he never asked for any.

Yet, the lessons showed to me by Tommy were priceless.

They are to this day.

# Young Guns

By 1995, most of The Young Guns and I had graduated from high school when my dad coincidentally retired from the United States Air Force.

He intensified his involvement in my music and in me, as both had become one and the same, then as now. He booked my band to our first shows beyond the city limits. In my exciting and naive days, those short journeys seemed like my last stop before the big time.

Dad was my manager, booking agent, van driver and sometimes, sound engineer.

We performed all over the southeastern United States, focusing mostly on Georgia, Florida and Alabama.

"We carried $5,000 worth of instruments and equipment inside a $5,000 van to sometimes drive 500 miles to earn $500 divided five ways."

That's an old slogan about musicians. It was also our life story in one sentence.

Believe me, we had no need for income tax shelters.

Until I moved to Nashville in 1998, my dad was my co-dreamer of someday becoming a major league entertainer. That's fatherly love in overdrive.

During my teenage years, my life was good. I had opportunities usually reserved only for adults. But I had few adult responsibilities. I had no wife, no children, no mortgage, no major debts and no health problems. I was a man and his music playing for people whose applause showed they liked it. The more I played before live audiences, the more I wanted to play larger ones.

And I thrived on moving from show to show, even inside that crowded van.

"Moving is the closest thing to being free," wrote Kris Kristofferson. The Young Guns and I were living that lyric, complete with the best kind of fun--spontaneous fun.

I learned a lesson about spontaneity being the birth of fun. I still believe that.

How much fun do you have when you obey an agenda? Consider a scheduled holiday or an appointment for a party. On such occasions, the implication is "have fun and do it now." But hearing an unexpected wisecrack, or encountering a surprising practical joke or suddenly winning a major award. Those things are always best when wrapped inside a surprise.

Around 1996, for example, the band and I played Gainesville, Florida, a college town.

We tried to "party" with some of the coeds, but to little avail. Some girls had little to do with minstrels traipsing throughout the South. Besides, my dad and another guy were with us. Their presence could put a damper on our teenage misbehavior. Still, the band and I had learned some traveling  savvy, and lessons pertaining to alcohol.

In a bar band, include some of your best music for the last set of the show. That's when bars' customers or owners buy musicians the most beer. The band (including some 17-year-olds) and I could usually score two six packs of free beer. Our scheme for scoring free beer should be filed in a library of life lessons for struggling musicians everywhere.

In Gainesville, after one final set, the band and I took our tired bodies to the motel, as usual. (In almost every town, the show's promoter subsidized two rooms for the entire group. The places were modest at best and dumps at worst.)

The musicians and I sauntered down a motel hallway ending abruptly by a plastic curtain stretching from the floor to the ceiling. We couldn't walk any farther, and didn't really care, as we'd reached our own rooms anyhow.

But we were curious as to why a plastic wall hung as the centerpiece of a busy hallway. Didn't the curtain prevent lodgers from getting to their rooms?

The next morning, we inquired about the flimsy barricade. A desk clerk told us that part of the motel was closed after an unwanted guest stayed there.

"What did he do?" I thought. "I hope he wasn't expelled for underage drinking of beer."

"He must have really acted up," said someone else in the band.

"No," said the desk clerk. "This motel's management wonders if he murdered a woman in that part of the hall, or inside a nearby room."

"What!?" said one of the guys. "A nearby room might mean next to where WE slept last night. Did you ever catch the guy?"

"We did, said the clerk," but not until he was arrested and police determined his earlier whereabouts all over the country, including a room inside that closed-off hallway.

"Do you remember his name?" continued someone.

"Ted Bundy," said the clerk.

It was THE Ted Bundy, the serial maniac who was convicted of murdering 36 women, and was suspected of killing more than 100!

Bundy died in 1989, seven years before the band and I slept in that motel. He had walked the hall that we walked. He'd passed by our two rooms, perhaps many times. He could have killed a victim inside the hall, or inside a room next to ours, then taken her body elsewhere. Committing murder in one place then moving the body to another was sometimes Bundy's Modus Operandi or M.O.

We often returned to that same town and nightclub. But we refused to stay in that motel.

## Beer

The general public has no idea how making music while riding nightly from town to town is a crash course in life lessons, whether or not the student wants them. The seeds of some of those lessons are planted in serious thinking during late-night, road-weary boredom.

But much of the wisdom is birthed by beer.

Most touring entertainers should have learned the brand of savvy known as common sense when they were youngsters, but they resisted. That's because traveling musicians are children at heart. They don't grow up for a reason. They don't have to.

You can get away with that free-spirited life because you have an excuse. You're earning a living for yourself and your dependents. Little things like deadlines and appointments don't matter when you're anticipating the next town and someone is driving you there on time.

I'm not that irresponsible today.

My dad and his tough love taught me the importance of realities, such as leaving a place on time to get to another place on time. His lesson was simple but necessary, and came when I was a teenager.

The band and I were returning from Rehoboth Beach, Delaware, where we'd opened for a "Doo-Wop" band from the 1960s. We stopped in Fayetteville, North Carolina, for an emergency.

We were out of beer.

By now, my dad obviously knew that I drank beer, and he didn't condone it. But he knew I'd sneak the stuff anyway, and he didn't want deceit between him and me. I'm glad he kept hypocrisy out of our relationship.

Dad reminded the band that he had an important meeting scheduled the next day in Georgia. He therefore didn't want to stop at all.

But band members and I assured Dad that we'd get up early so he could keep his appointment if he'd simply let us spend the night in Fayetteville and its brew.

"Fine," he said. "But the van will pull out at 7 a.m. Each of you guys better be on it."

Perhaps he knew all along that we'd likely fail to get up on time, and that he'd teach us a lesson in punctuality. It worked.

That night, my buddies and I drank all of our beer. Due to the late hour, stores wouldn't sell more. So we set our room clock, and passed out on the beds and floor.

Someone heard the alarm, and someone turned it off. He and the rest of us wanted a few more minutes sleep before facing a throbbing hangover.

When we didn't get up, my dad pounded our room's door with the force of a jackhammer. Everyone inside ignored the racket.

Dad rang our room's telephone, and said the van was leaving at 7 a.m.

"If he actually departs, how will we ever get home," I wondered?

That seemed like a question worthy of continued sleep.

All of us returned to that very thing.

"After all, Dad wouldn't really leave five guys with no money on foot a few hundred miles from home," I assumed. "I mean, he's a nice guy, right? Nice guys wouldn't forsake their son and his cronies."

Wrong.

Suddenly, I heard the unmistakable sound of the band's oil-burning van. It was pulling out of the driveway.

I saw its brake lights brighten, a turn signal activate, and its wheels turn toward home. It was out of sight in seconds.

THAT got us to awaken.

I don't recall how we thought we were going to subsidize bus tickets. Perhaps we thought we could score free tickets the way we often scored beer. Who knows?

Afraid we'd miss the bus, just as we'd already missed the van, we grabbed our gear and instruments and began wrestling everything down the interstate. We didn't take time to shower or fully dress. Passers-by had to wonder why some of us were in our pajamas.

Then, like a rainbow after a storm, we happily saw our van parked outside a Shoney's Restaurant.

Five musicians, some rubbing their sleepy eyes, darted among speeding cars to get to Dad's van.

Drivers were honking and cussing.

We staggered into the Shoney's lot where there was no time for breakfast. Dad's appointment was still approaching. The musicians and I collapsed inside the van. The trip home before the next trip to a venue was again underway. Excepting Dad and his friend, everyone fell asleep. No one thought about beer.

To this day, I rarely miss scheduled departures.

# Know-Know

Thoroughly know your employer as well as your employees. I recommend that lesson to anyone in any business, including musicians. Reading that rule here is much easier than learning it from real-world experience. I can attest to that.

A touring musician without a recording contract performs a lot of cover tunes. I know that from my early days of touring. Know your crowd and its tastes before you go on stage.

The Young Guns and I had landed a three-night booking in Gadsden, Alabama, at the Fuzzy Duck, a hip nightclub. Three nights meant we could play in one town instead of rushing to two more in two days. We loved that.

I was approached by the club's owner after the first set. I smelled whisky on his breath before he ever spoke.

"Play Prince's 'Purple Rain,'" he somewhat slurred.

Politely, I told him we were a country band, and the song wasn't in our set list.

In minutes, we took the stage to begin our next show. Lo-and-behold, the owner stationed himself right in front of the bandstand. He loudly demanded again and again that we play "Purple Rain."

I preferred a black eye. His.

Instead, I kept playing.

He became a real distraction, and tried to yell over the music.

But I had a microphone, so I could yell even louder.

I told him we didn't know the song.

I said, "F--k the Fuzzy Duck."

It's never a good idea to tell off a nightclub owner in front of his crowd. At the end of the set, I was fired before I could quit.

The Young Guns and I were fired another time, this time after our first set on the first night of a two-week engagement!

One of my employees was to blame.

He, like everyone else in the band, was excited about the job because it sat across the street from a topless nightclub.

Some of the band had already met a few of the women who worked there. The guys were in the "mood" to meet the dancers, and thought they'd definitely form friendships during 14-days of interacting with them after each show.

Besides, it was Christmastime, and we were booked through New Year's Eve. People are always more giving during those holidays.

We hoped those women would be too.

The New Year's Eve show paid a double scale.

For this special run, I decided to hire a fiddle player, a good musician from the mountains from North Georgia. I never thought that someone with rural raising would know much about nighttime women.

I was wrong.

After we played our set, the fiddle player asked a waitress if she'd like to fiddle around. She went for it, and the two hid inside a broom closet at the back of the dance floor.

There, they made their own brand of music.

Suddenly, the club manager opened the door and saw the naked truth. That was a problem, especially since the woman was his girlfriend!

Employers hate employees who have sex with their girlfriends. That's a lesson I didn't need to learn that night.

I'd just assumed it since childhood.

The band and I were fired with no opportunity to seriously interact with the ladies in the topless bar. They might have been more refined than women inside broom closets.

# Bars

Few things reflect American culture more than its nightclubs. In a bar, every economic group comes together. By and large, everyone is treated equally, and there's little class distinction.

The latest fashions, dances, music and food are found in bars. Even backwoods country bars with outdated music on a worn out jukebox will have a new fishing lure or a shotgun shell on the wall, or maybe a bass or catfish that someone recently caught in a nearby stream or, some girl's fashionable brassiere.

One décor change the band and I have noticed since 2010 is that many working-class and middle-class bars are at least partially decorated with posters from "Duck Dynasty," a huge television show and corporate franchise.

The Young Guns and I first realized a more troubling change in bars' trends in the 1990s when more and more nightclubs began hiring less and less live music. Those taverns switched to recorded music, often with disc jockeys and karaoke. Then, in the 2000s, the karaoke foothold intensified as records became background accompaniment for almost anybody who wanted to sing publicly.

Touring bands began to dissolve because they had no place to play.

But thank goodness it wasn't that way for the Guns and me. The fact that we were still in demand told me that we'd been doing our music pretty well.

Granted, we only earned around five hundred to seven hundred dollars a night. We were still paying for our own gasoline and food, and sometimes even for our motel rooms. (Now you understand why we hustled free beer!)

So it was nice to settle in for a two-night date in Stockbridge, Georgia. We could play as long as we wanted, and stay up until we fell asleep, as we didn't have to drive hundreds of miles before the next night's show.

But this show, like all the others, would exhibit its own personality.

At first, the owner showed us a lot of hospitality, with free hamburgers and French fries. His friendliness was characteristic, and no wonder. We'd made a lot of money for him on previous engagements.

We thought we'd return his kindness. We'd use our new soundboard for the very first time. His customers would be the first to ever hear its crisp audio, or so we thought.

We arrived well in advance of our 9 p.m. starting time. As we began our sound check, someone activated the new board, and smoke poured out everywhere. Someone dashed for a fire extinguisher. A handful of people sprinted toward the doors.

No one had told us that a customer had rewired the stage's electrical outlets. After consuming too many alcoholic beverages, he had wired the outlets to 220 volts, not the standard 110 volts.

Simply put, the double voltage turned into a fire that went up like a paper match.

Nothing starts a show better than a bonfire in the middle of the room.

My dad went to the nightclub's owner to explain that The Young Guns and I wouldn't be able to play that night. The owner was not happy. People who come to a live music club don't stay if there's no live music, so many left.

The next day, the band, my dad and I found an old soundboard that belonged to a nearby friend. We hooked it up, and played our standard four sets.

At the evening's end, all of us were mentally fried, just as we usually were after a show.

Dad went into the owner's office to collect our fee for the the weekend. The owner refused to pay for the night we couldn't play.

He said we should also have played the final night's songs free of charge because we hadn't played at all the previous night.

"We didn't play last night because we had no soundboard because your 'electrician' wired the place all wrong," Dad argued. "It's his fault, or your fault, that we couldn't play. But we asked for no money."

"But as for tonight," Dad continued. "We DID play, and we want to be paid for this night."

No avail. The owner didn't budge. He didn't want to pay.

"Okay," said Dad. "I'll go get five exhausted, hot-headed teenage musicians to come into this office. I'll let you explain to all of them why they're not going to get paid."

Things could have gotten really tense, or totally out of hand. But we got paid for one night, which was half of what we'd originally expected to make.

The owner was yelling at the band and me as we left his club. He kept insisting that things would be *different* the next time we played his place.

We told him they'd definitely be different, as we wouldn't come back. And we never did.

We lost a regular, feeding and paying job just because someone wired the place wrong. That club's personality, and the fate behind it, had changed against us. The way I see it, everyone involved was a loser due to circumstances beyond everyone's control.

I learned, once again, that was just life on the road.

# 10

# Angela and Mark

In 1996, not long after I graduated high school, my dad shared another piece of his timeless wisdom. I adopted it as a lesson that I use to this day.

"Trust the people you meet through people you already trust," he said.

Dad and Vivian had met Mark and Angela Pitts at Nashville South, the nightclub the Young Guns and I played many times in Macon.

Dad often noticed the Pitts at a table situated directly in front of the bandstand. Even though they lived in Americus, Georgia, a tiny town 74 miles from Macon, they always came to Nashville South whenever the band and I played there. In those days, the Pitts were the most loyal fans I had.

"I'd call ahead and reserve the table in front of the bandstand," Angela recalled in 2015. "People would come to our table and ask to sit with Mark and me. The next thing I knew, there were ten to twenty people. We were known as the 'Party Crowd,' and we earned it."

More and more, Dad and I began to talk to the Pitts. They were the perfect example of Southern friendliness and hospitality.

Once we knew each other fairly well, when I would go to various concerts in Buena Vista, Georgia, near the Pitts' home in Americus, they let me stay at their house. It was great because I didn't have to drive all night back to Macon after the shows.

Dad trusted the Pitts, and so did I. These great acquaintances became trusted friends. And quickly.

Dad asked Angela to sell our CD during my sets at Nashville South. The band and I had recorded a compact disc that included eight songs. Before too long, she and her husband were traveling with Dad, the band and me so she could sell more CDs.

Over time, Angela sold hundreds of copies for ten dollars apiece. At each night's end, she gave the money to my dad, as well as the CDs that weren't sold. These party people, whom I'd met in a bar, never once showed any discrepancies in the cash or inventory. Neither Angela nor Mark ever asked for a commission for selling the recordings. They were just helping their friends, a relatively unknown teenage band.

Dad had financed the recording of that self-produced CD. How many people would invest money in a project, and then let newcomers to their lives sell the inventory? But Dad was an excellent evaluator of personal character. He is to this day.

Soon, the Pitts were traveling with the Young Guns and me wherever we played, including Georgia, Florida and elsewhere throughout the Southeast. They'd arrive early at each nightclub to set up a merchandise stand featuring my CD.

The Pitts subsidized their own lodging, eating and incidentals as they traveled in the band's van, and sometimes in their own car.

The Pitts spent their own money to help a young band earn its own money.

Fans heard me make song dedications to the Pitts. People saw me go to their table after restroom breaks. They seemed fascinated by the way the Pitts "organized" lines of CD buyers, and the way Angela seemed to "know" everything that was happening about me, on and off the road. Virtually every weekend, she fielded questions about me, including when and where I'd play next. (I had no website in those days.)

Angela's activities began to resemble something like a fan club. So that's exactly what she became—the founder and president of my first official fan club.

By then, she was sending out newsletters, replenishing the CD stock and doing odd jobs related to my struggling career. Her involvement in my life became a fulltime job. That continued for almost three years.

Mark and Angela, the couple who'd never trifled with my cash flow, strongly refused to take a salary. I'm not sure, but I suspect the Pitts even paid for the postage for brochures Angela sent to fans in three states.

As I've indicated earlier in these pages, the band and I were driven by our love for music. A few close people were driven by their love for us. Mark and Angela were at the head of the line.

So it became a festive and fulfilling ritual...my dad, the Pitts, the band and me riding in a van and pulling a used trailer carrying instruments and sound equipment. We'd usually arrive at a venue in the afternoon, play three sets from 9 p.m. until 2 a.m., and wonder how we'd muster the energy to tear down all of the equipment, pack it up and ride to the next show where we'd repeat the routine. We'd be indescribably tired inside that van. Anyone wanting to sleep could usually do so, soundly, even while sitting upright with the radio blaring and others talking.

It was the hardest job we ever loved. All of us.

Angela recently remembered one trip that could have come out of a horror movie called "Never Try This at Home."

The family, friends, band and I were pulling the trailer from Macon to the Eastside Country Club in Albany, Georgia. The gig lasted from Wednesday through Friday night. After the Friday show, everyone in the exhausted group loaded the van and trailer to ride five hours to Savannah.

We'd not had any real sleep when we erected our equipment to play a 10 a.m., Saturday talent contest sponsored by Jimmy Dean Foods. The band members needed showers before going on stage.

We couldn't afford motel rooms for everyone, so we paid for only one room. We didn't need anything fancy, and apparently we picked a real dump. The idea was to take turns using the shower, then ride to the contest.

While somewhat asleep on my feet, I eased bare-footed into the shower stall and stepped on sharp chicken bones! They stuck me, and I came out of the stall yelling. Other chicken bones were under the sheets. No matter how weary, no one wanted to lie down.

Someone had rubber shower shoes. Others in the band wrapped towels around their feet to stand among the broken bones. My dad and the Pitts decided they didn't have time or desire to take a shower, and everyone understood why.

This story isn't over.

We won the Saturday morning contest, and loaded up again to drive five more hours back to Albany. There, we tore down our gear after the show and arrived back in Macon after daylight Sunday.

Through all of that, my dad did most of the driving. The Pitts ran my CD stand.

That tour's final morning ended in Macon where all of us went our separate ways. But not before everyone asked when and where we'd do our next show.

Through it all, I'd seen firsthand the value of trusting people who were recommended by trustworthy people.

My dad lifted me up at an early age.

I'm age two, looking for my first grand slam.

Three generations. My dad, Barry, me and Grandpa Aldine Williams

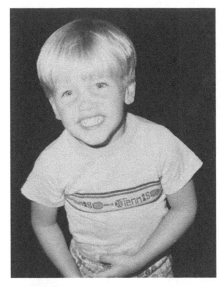

This is my wrestling face.

Early picture of my mom, Debbie, and me.

My dad's band during the 1980's; from L-R  Johnny Johnson, Barry Williams, Ray Williams, Fred Treadway

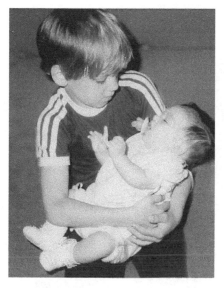

My baby sister, Kasi, was born in 1984. I was seven.

Cousin Papo (12), Kasi (3) and Jason (10)

Kasi and me, ages three and ten.

My first band, The Young Guns, and me.

An early publicity
photo. I'm age 18.

Here's my senior picture taken in 1995.

Me before my signature goatee.

My buddy, Tommy Powell. I sang to him in a Pepsi truck.

Benny Brown, President of Broken Bow Records,
gave me my record deal.

Here I am with Michael Knox, the creator of my recorded
musical sound.

Michael Knox and me celebrating the sale of 2,000,000 units of "My Kinda Party."

Backstage in Charlotte, NC with Vivian and my dad.

Kasi and me at my
engagement party.
Brittany said "Yes!"

Dad and me at my
wedding in Mexico.

My mom, Debbie,
and me.

A night out with Keeley, Brittany and Kendyl.

A family gathering. From L-R: Dad, Vivian, Brittany, Kendyl, me, Keeley, and Debbie (Mom) and David Wood

The most kick-ass band on the planet. L-R: Jay Jackson,
Jack Sizemore, Tully Kennedy, Rich Redmond and Kurt Allison

Jay Jackson

Jack Sizemore

Tully Kennedy

Rich Redmond

Kurt Allison

Jason Aldean, 2016 and 2017 Academy of Country Music's Entertainer of the Year.

# 11

# Michael

Earlier in these pages I said that persistence has been an unfailing life lesson for me. Through Michael Knox, vice president at Nashville's Warner-Chappell Music, I took that lesson a step further.

I learned the value of persistence when people put their faith in people—imperfect people—the only kind God ever made.

Michael had faith in me. During events that I couldn't predict, no one else in Nashville shared Michael's passionate belief in me. He sometimes had more faith in me than I had in myself.

In 1998, I'd never heard of Warner-Chappell Music. I was still living the dream in Macon, Georgia, and had little familiarity with Nashville's music business structure.

I'd also never heard of Michael Knox. But God or fate or both sent Michael to Macon to visit his grandmother.

I didn't know her either.

I also had no idea that Michael, a music executive, was scouting for a specific country music "voice." He wanted a vocal sound that could ease through a George Strait ballad just as effortlessly as it could blast Bob Seger's rock'n'roll. He wanted a sensitive voice, mixed with power and projected with edge, Michael said years later. And he wanted that same singer to have stage presence that was natural, even if the "natural" didn't meet conformity.

I'm glad I didn't know all of that at the time. I might have told Michael I didn't know anyone like that.

In time, he said he found those things in me.

A few days earlier, Michael had received an email from the manager of The Buckboard, a north Atlanta nightclub. The email was promoting a two-night talent contest, and asked Michael to attend.

I'd be the 17th of 20 artists in the show. But my name was of no particular interest to Michael. He'd never heard of me, nor anyone else in the contest.

In addition to his role at Warner-Chappell, Michael was also a great music producer and historian. The son of rock'n'roll pioneer Buddy Knox ("Party Doll" 1957), Michael didn't just listen to music; he "heard" it, breaking down the tempo, instrumentation and chord structures.

The first time Michael heard me, he instantly recognized that many of my songs' chord progressions were straight-on rock music.

Following my Buckboard set, I spoke briefly to Michael. After I learned he was in the music business, I gave him a compact disc I'd recorded on my first visit to Nashville two years earlier. It was a low budget CD that no one will ever mistake as a masterpiece, not then or now.

Michael spent two days with his grandmother without listening to my music. But on the way back to Nashville, he played my CD in his car and played the entire thing without finding much that interested him.

Except for one song—"Cowboy Lady."

As soon as he returned to Nashville, Michael called me. I couldn't have been more excited if I'd been contacted by the President.

He asked where I'd be playing next. I told him and he came. He then sent me some songs he wanted me to learn. He came to see me a third time just to see how I'd interpreted his tunes.

I didn't rise to his hopes. I was stressing out on stage. I even forgot the words to one of his songs.

Michael called my dad who was still my manager. He told Dad that he believed in me, but he said that each time I performed I was less impressive than the previous time.

Still, he told my dad, it was time for me to take a giant leap of faith, and give up my "day job" to move to Nashville. He told Dad he wanted to help me become a recording artist under his direction.

What if Michael had said he was through with me? What if his disappointment in my performances meant he was mistaken the first night I impressed him?

If that had happened, you wouldn't have heard my seven albums that have produced 17 number-one songs.

Instead, as I continued to underwhelm him in performing, Michael ignored his discontent and instead relied upon his original intuition. He reminded himself that first impressions are not only the most lasting, they're also usually correct. That was one of the life lessons Michael had learned through his experiences.

I adopted that lesson for myself and I use it to this day.

In August 2015 Broken Bow Records threw a "Number-One Party" for me to celebrate three songs that had risen to the top slot from just one album. I spoke to the few hundred people who attended the celebration. I told them that I almost always trust my first impressions, even if they involve risk.

Looking across the sea of faces, I could tell that some folks thought I was crazy.

Overall, I think too many people spend too much time analyzing. When they do that, they're trying to talk themselves out of something, not into it.

They shouldn't do that, not when it applies to music.

Making music is a creative process. Creativity is about feelings, not logic. So when I KNOW I'm feeling something, I'm going to chase it. And I'm going to stand by it. And I don't care if it's risky. And I don't care who cares.

Michael Knox taught me that lesson. My own experiences prove it.

# No Hurry

P er Michael Knox's repeated advice, I took that leap of faith and quit my job with Pepsi-Cola in Macon and moved to Nashville.

Michael put me in "artist development" at Warner-Chappell. The intention was to make me a successful recording artist. He made sure I had a modest amount of money by paying me advances-against-royalties up to $13,000 annually to write songs.

At some point I was told that Warner-Chappell usually fires songwriters if they don't generate income by the time their advances reach $100,000. Michael kept my yearly income low so I could stay for seven and a half years, even if I didn't earn for the company.

All the time, Michael and I were chasing the dream—to develop an original sound and then find a label that would record and market it.

Both became giant challenges. But whenever I was discouraged, Michael's non-stop enthusiasm inspired me.

We went into the studio during my early Nashville days to record songs written by Jeff Stevens, Steve Bogart and Marv Green. They'd written a lot of hits for George Strait.

But Michael disliked their songs when I sung them.

"Those melodies were working," Michael said recently. "But Jason didn't have the right energy. It wasn't where we needed to be."

Then one day, I wrote "Where Did I Go Wrong."

"Dude," Michael said, smiling. "This song is where we need to be."

To this day, Michael says that song launched the Jason Aldean groove that triggered my eventual "sound."

"It had that cool little energy," Michael said. "It had a little bit of an aggressive vibe that was not current at the time."

In the 1990s, "Where Did I Go Wrong" wasn't a radio hit. But it was a quiet hit on Nashville's Music Row, that neighborhood where hit songs are written, produced and distributed. Suddenly, music business insiders were buzzing about Michael and that guy from Macon he believed in so much.

However slowly, Michael and I were off to the races. Now, I thought, the artist development team at Warner-Chappell could throw my development into fast gear.

But my thought was too little too late. The artist development folks weren't interested.

I had earlier signed a record deal at Capitol Records. I don't discuss it that much because the contract was in name only.

So Capitol wasn't around when Michael and I finally got the sound that we wanted . . . the sound we'd shop to record companies throughout Nashville.

Without a development team, Michael and I were two guys flying solo but not for long.

"It doesn't matter who jumped ship," Michael said to me. "So what if we're alone? We now have something (*Where Did I Go Wrong*.) And we're going to go from here."

And we did. During the process, I learned a bunch of lessons from my friend and teacher Michael Knox.

First of all, I realized I had no idea he'd been secretly developing me in my way at my pace. Therefore, I realized that in life a person can throw punches without announcing each blow.

"The hardest thing in the world when you are developing an artist is to not trick them into doing what you want them to do," Michael recalls. "Instead, let them find that path of what they really are. Because we took the time, Jason grew into an attitude. He had his own visions too. I just tried to raise his expectations higher. That's the reason why we have a Reba. That's the reason we have a Garth. Inside, they had something. You, as a developer, have to be patient enough and not tell them what to do and to let them learn their process of releasing what's creative inside of them."

I didn't know all of that at the time. Or, if I did, I didn't realize it then as much as I do today, thanks to Michael.

Once again, I learned a life lesson by absorbing someone else's.

Today, I don't force anybody who's pursuing creativity to hurry. And I don't force myself to hurry, not in my career or in my life. If anyone has that "it" factor in his or her mind and soul, it will present itself in its own way and in its own time.

I practice that lesson from Michael all the time. Development isn't a goal, it's a lifestyle. And it doesn't quit, not if you freely let it grow.

I feel sorry for the current crop of rising recording artists. Today's record labels don't let them develop. Instead, the record companies look for good singers to match with good songs in search of a radio and digital hit. If it happens, they do it again. And again and again until the singer's body of work becomes stale and predictable.

Once the public can predict you, it will abandon you.

I've often had resistance from people on my career team. One of their frequent criticisms about a new album is that it doesn't sound like the last one.

"Thank you!" I say, sometimes to myself, sometimes out loud.

Because at that point, I know that my inner creativity is alive and well. And I know that my "sound" is just what I want it to be.

My sound will always be predictably unpredictable. I love that. And because I do, the fans love it, too. Know why?

Because love is contagious, whether in romance, parenting or standing by that silent voice saying you're doing your craft the right way.

Your own way.

# Tully

Despite its value, persistence isn't the only requirement you need in order to fulfill your dreams. You must also be mentally and emotionally tough.

You have to be tough when the going gets rough.

More than ever, I began to realize that in 1999 as I my struggle in Nashville continued a year after my arrival.

With little success, I had performed for several record label executives and music producers. Michael and I had largely established a vocal sound, but not a signature instrumental sound to his liking. That began to change when Michael introduced me to bass guitarist Tully Kennedy.

He'd been playing bass around Nashville since January of 1997, one year before I'd arrived. Tully wore an armor of toughness that I didn't learn about until we became friends.

That toughness—that brand of intensity—feeds determination that feeds persistence. All the while, Tully kept his mental toughness—leather toughness—and he refused to let life and its circumstances beat him down. While awaiting a career "break," he shared dumpy apartments, drove junk cars and ate the cheapest fast foods, if he ate at all. Once, he had absolutely no money. Not one cent. He pressed forward, and played his show that night anyway.

Tully could have returned to his upstate New York home where he'd played in twenty bands. But the move would translate into a boring job that only guaranteed essentials like food, clothing and housing. Afterwards, he'd have wondered for the rest of his life what would have happened had he stayed in Nashville while going for the big-time. For him, the big-time was to have regular work as a studio musician.

That was his plan, and there was no Plan B.

"I've learned that you have to chase your dreams," he said. "Your dreams sure won't chase you."

That was a lesson that I'd known for years. I just hadn't put it into those exact words.

So Tully hung on during many bleak years. He nourished his passion to play bass guitar, and to play it with the best musicians he could find. He was tough. Physical hunger or a shady place to live didn't stop him.

I'd eventually learn that before he and I met, he'd played every dive on lower Broadway, once a rough and tumble neighborhood of rundown bars, pawn shops, massage parlors, adult movie shops and hookers. (Today, lower Broadway is a high-profile, popular tourist destination.)

While still struggling, Tully played Printer's Alley, which was once a sparkling Nashville neighborhood of nightclubs built in the 1940s, named for the printing shops housed in the alley some 60 years earlier. In its prime, Printer's Alley resembled a miniature Bourbon Street in New Orleans.

Today, only a few nightclubs remain. Most were lost to modern expansion. Where there once were bars, restaurants and theaters, now there is a boutique hotel, condominiums and high-dollar eateries.

When Tully worked Printer's Alley, he caught the beginning of the end of the Alley's festive days. A few marquees were dented, and a number of neon lights were broken or burned out, much like some of the people who owned them.

One such place was Skull's Rainbow Room, owned by the late David "Skull" Schulman. Tully went there occasionally to play his bass and hoped that each gig might lead to a better one.

Tully thought he was close to the big-time when he landed a job at Tootsie's Orchard Lounge, popularly called the "world's most famous honky-tonk." Tootsie's has expanded to additional locations in the United States. In fact, when visitors depart at Nashville International Airport, one of the first things they see is another Tootsie's restaurant and bar, complete with autographed photographs of country music legends, just like it is in the original Tootsie's downtown.

The original Tootsie's sits directly across the alley from the Ryman Auditorium, the home of the Grand Ole Opry from 1943 until 1974. Johnny Cash, Dolly Parton, Willie Nelson, Waylon Jennings, Roger Miller, Patsy Cline and scores of other country stars patronized Tootsie's. Countless hit songs were written there, where the walls are laced with celebrity pictures, autographs, beer stains, cigarette burns, lipstick and other souvenirs.

So Tully thought that working Tootsie's was one step away from exposure to the power brokers on Nashville's nearby Music Row. He was thrilled, but not for long.

He was astonished and deflated when told he'd be paid $16.00 for his twelve-hour shifts, beginning at 2 p.m. and ending at 2 a.m.

"I was accustomed to earning five hundred to seven hundred dollars for three nights a week back home," Tully said. "That wasn't too bad in the early 1990s. So when I got a job at Tootsie's, I obviously thought I'd make that much money or more."

His salary was less than minimum wage, far less than a pizza deliveryman's or a lawn boy's. But he did what he always did, and toughed out the marathon shifts. He often split his earnings between a little gasoline and a little food.

Tully played other Nashville rooms, including Legends Corner. Fistfights were common. He thinks that one of those joints had chicken wire hanging between the band and customers. The barrier was to prevent people from throwing bottles at the musicians.

I've heard Tully's stories about Nashville's rough and rowdy joints where women flirted with men, and men belted other men.

His recollections reminded me of places I'd played during my high school days and after my graduation. At age 14, when Tully was too young to drive, his mother took him to bars to play music, just like mine had. His parents had divorced when he was two, mine when I was three. Tully and I share a mutual personal history of toughness against our struggles.

Tully met Michael Knox through Tully's uncle, Roy Hurd, a songwriter for Warner-Chappell. Michael wanted to form a band whose members would understand the kind of sound he and I wanted.

So he introduced Tully to me.

He played with me for years before I got my record deal at Broken Bow Records. We played countless showcases and were consistently turned down.

"Playing a showcase is actually playing for people looking for a reason *not* to sign you to a record deal," Tully said. "They don't know what they want; they just think they'll know it when they hear it. You have to be tough to play those things time after time. Some of those people watch you play for an hour, then never even get back to you."

After six years of playing together, "Hicktown" became my first Top Ten song. Tully was still my bass player and he is to this day. He's played bass on all of my records, and has toured with me into giant coliseums and arenas in America and overseas.

But even after "Hicktown," Tully's attitude remained as tough as the rest of the band's and mine. Our first hit song didn't shoot us into the headlines. We instead opened shows for other groups, some of whom we'd never heard. We played gigs where no one even listened, including people at motocross competitions. Ever try to get attention above the roar of 30 motorcycles?

And we didn't make any real money right away, either. Tully said that in those days not one of us ever had more than $100.00.

We continued playing small or out-of-the-way venues like those from our most financially desperate days. We even played empty bars, sometimes for little money, other times just to keep the band tight.

Tully remembered that "Hicktown" was regularly heard on the radio when we played Coyote Joe's in North Carolina, a saloon with only one customer that night. One!

But we played with intensity, as if we were playing Madison Square Garden. You have to really love your music and let toughness kill your personal problems when you're performing a song destined to launch your career for one, lone, solitary man.

Who knows? Perhaps the guy had undergone difficult times, like everyone else. If so, he could have learned about toughening up by listening to Tully.

# Rich

Rich Redmond, my drummer, may not have been the originator of my life's lessons. But he has confirmed a few.

When I was in my twenties, I felt the same as a lot of people do about personal relationships. I thought compatibility was formed by people's mutual interests. But maturity has taught me something different.

For example, Rich, one of my closest friends, has no interest in sports. I'm a sports fanatic. Rich moves at two speeds, fast and faster. I like to work hard at my craft, then work slowly at relaxing.

I doubt Rich has ever killed anything in his life. I was thrilled after recently killing a 32-point buck. Rich prefers the city where he can rush to various business appointments. I prefer to stroll quietly among my 1,500 wooded acres.

And I love it. I feel like I'm closer to God when I'm by myself among His creation. It's a brand of solitude that's a mild form of therapy all of us need, but usually don't take the time to get. As one of my most tireless life lessons, I urge people to hurry when it's appropriate, then when it's time, relax with the same dedication.

Good ol' Rich simply can't rest when he's relaxing. He *always* attacks life. Meanwhile, I'm happy to simply absorb it.

I've learned that compatibility doesn't always require mutual ideas or behavior. Compatibility starts with respecting someone who totally lives the way he wants and achieves happiness while doing so.

That's Rich.

He's one of those rare people who has mastered his craft and lifestyle with integrity. He says what he'll do, and he does what he says.

I watch Rich exhibit that behavior from day to day.

I see him tirelessly chase the fulfillment of his dreams.

It reminds me of the years when I chased mine. Ironically, Rich is one of the people who helped me reach my goals. He played drums behind me at Nashville showcases for record labels. He played again and again when twenty labels said "no" before one said "yes."

Who wouldn't be drawn to his passionate perseverance?

He began playing drums in 1977 at age seven. Encouraged by his father (like I was encouraged by mine), Rich advanced quickly, and was shortly enrolled at the Milford Percussion and Guitar Workshop in Milford, Connecticut. He had a blue sparkle snare drum and a pawnshop bass drum as his first equipment.

My first instrument was that cheap guitar mentioned earlier in these pages.

At age 11, Rich moved with his parents to Texas, a state with many good musical programs. As you know, I moved back and forth from Georgia and Florida during my childhood.

Rich joined the concert band, orchestra, jazz ensemble, pep bands and bands outside of his public school! Not me. I stayed with my preferred music or baseball, nothing else. In the 9th grade, he joined his school's marching band. Pursuing only one musical outlet wasn't enough for Rich.

I've heard my friend Reba McEntire often say that no one will succeed at anything unless he or she is passionate about it. Unbeknownst to Reba, she was reciting a thumbnail sketch of Rich and his childhood.

But it didn't stop there.

By the time he graduated from high school, Rich had decided to pursue music professionally. He attended Texas Tech University for four years. He then attended the University of North Texas where he earned a Masters Degree in Music Education.

The entire time he was in school, he often worked nights and weekends at Dallas nightclubs playing music.

All the while, he wasn't afraid to dream big.

So he traveled to Nashville from Texas because he'd heard that Trisha Yearwood was auditioning drummers. He sent a demo tape to her people. They replied that 15 other drummers had also responded.

"But you can be the sixteenth guy," Rich was told.

Competition culled the list, and Rich was one of the final two competitors.

"But the other guy lived in Nashville so he got the job," Rich said.

The same scenario went down with Deana Carter and Barbara Mandrell.

Rich actually financed three roundtrip airplane tickets to Nashville because his self-confidence told him he was qualified to play in anybody's band, including a national celebrity's. Three times he was disappointed. But not once was he discouraged.

"So I realized I'd never make it in music unless I moved to New York City or Los Angeles or Nashville," Rich said. "I didn't want to go to New York; I didn't know anyone in L.A. so I moved to Nashville. I knew a few people there from having worked those three auditions."

He took the leap, and pulled into Nashville with little more than music in his soul and dreams in his eyes.

When I learned about that stunt, I realized how much Rich and I had identical attitudes and obsessions. And when he played, it came from his heart by way of lean times.

Get this. Without money and with few contacts, Rich was desperate for cash flow. So he took a job waiting tables (in a restaurant that now happens to be a drugstore). How many people with a Master's degree want something so badly they'll serve food in a town full of tourists? Rich had to please hurried customers wanting to race to the next attraction.

Little did his customers know that while Rich was feeding their stomachs, he was simultaneously feeding his dream.

Rich Redmond, the higher education graduate, conspicuously carried dinner plates while secretly toting a telephone pager.

If it buzzed, Rich abandoned his customers long enough to return the call at a pay phone. He'd often accept an invitation to play later that night. For a whopping thirty dollars and free beer, the man who almost became Trisha Yearwood's drummer occasionally played five 60-minute sets in one night.

"But you know what?" he recalls. "I played every one of those jobs as if I were playing Madison Square Garden. I formed relationships that led to more relationships. And eventually I played the real Madison Square Garden."

About this time, Rich met Tully Kennedy who introduced him to guitarist Kurt Allison, the three guys who played on my first album for Broken Bow Records. Since then, they've played on every record I've ever recorded, and at every show I've ever performed.

Today, that band and I do about 85 dates a year, meaning we're on the road more than 100 days annually. So Rich has finally satisfied his long-sought ambition and fulfilled his dreams. Right? No. Not at all.

He's now host to "Drummer's Weekend," an annual instructional drum playing conference. He teaches "CRASH," a motivational program that he presents to schools and Fortune 500 companies across the country. Rich is the author of

*FUNdamentals of Drumming for Kids*, an international best-selling how-to book on drumming for young people.

On some days, only hours before playing a concert with me, Rich holds classes in the city where the band and I are performing. He also keeps busy recording with the band and me at sessions between dates on our touring schedule.

Rich has appeared in a motion picture and wants to play in others. He's taking voice acting lessons to learn how to perform many voices for radio and television commercials.

He must be the busiest musician in Nashville.

I marvel at his high-powered daily agenda, and I'm thankful for the life lessons behind Rich's consistency, stamina and his determination to meet new people.

"New people become old relationships," he says. "And in the entertainment industry, relationships are vital."

I agree. And although Rich and I do not have many common interests, we share our careers and music as priorities.

But I still get a charge out of killing a 32-point buck!

# 15

# Kelly

One of my most important lessons has been to consolidate my life lessons. Lessons are usually taught one at a time. But I don't pull out a single thought each time I face a new situation. After all, memories aren't individually packed inside a filing cabinet.

Instead, the more thoughts you assemble in your mind, the more they combine to become your personality, mind and soul.

From my dad, my mom, Michael Knox, members of my band and myself, I've tried to master the art of fair play.

"Treat people the way you want to be treated," is one of those overall lessons. That may seem trite, but it isn't.

People won't always remember what you say or sing. But they'll always remember how you made them feel.

That one lesson will simplify complex situations in anybody's life. I know. I've seen it in others, as well as in myself.

I think that treating people as you'd like to be treated was behind "Don't You Wanna Stay," my recorded duet with Kelly Clarkson.

Kelly wasn't signed to my record label. She and I don't share the same personal manager. Those factors often comprise the "politics" of duets in Nashville's music industry.

I didn't care about that stuff. I asked Kelly to sing with me because she's a great singer. I'd found the right song, she had the right voice and we did the record. It was just that simple.

Why allow a professional situation to complicate an idea born from a whisper inside your creative mind?

I believe first inclinations are like first impressions. They're the most lasting, and the most accurate.

For example, I briefly considered Miranda Lambert, but she'd already sung background on one of my albums, "Reckless." Carrie Underwood's name came up, too.

Both of those women are talented singers and fine entertainers. They have mastered their craft. But considering them proved to be wrong for that particular song.

I returned to Kelly's big, soulful voice with its cool rasp. When she sings, it's effortless. To top it off, she has one of the most engaging personalities I've ever encountered.

Remember how I told you that I can assess a crowd in the first 30 seconds of my live shows? I knew I'd selected the right singer during my first minute with her in the studio.

The night before the session, I made notes of helpful hints for Kelly on how to sing "Don't You Wanna Stay." My preparations were a waste of time.

I'd thought Kelly and I should rehearse our parts because I wanted her to be comfortable with the tune. So I started singing the song, and she began singing the part I wanted her to sing. She nailed it—and her singing was incredible.

I threw away my notes. I don't think she ever saw them. Meanwhile, our duet became a giant hit record. It was nominated for the Academy of Country Music's "Vocal Event of the Year."

That's the good news. But during the summer of 2015, an entertainment story broke saying that Kelly couldn't find a duet partner. She said no one wanted to sing with her because she'd gained weight. I was outraged when I heard the news.

She's a singer, not a size-two fashion model. And anybody who rebuffs her because of her weight isn't searching for good music. They're practicing ugly discrimination. And there's nothing in discrimination that's pleasing to the ear or good for the soul.

Today, if I found another duet that I thought would fit, I'd ask Kelly to sing with me in a minute. I love the largeness of her voice, and have no interest in her waistline.

Regrettably, that thought prompts another of life's many lessons that are painfully learned by all of us. The lesson is: some people are just dumb, especially when they wrongfully discriminate. And some of those people are actually meaner than they are dumb.

# 16

On May 2, 2010, the band and I finished a show in Canada and started watching television and Internet coverage of heavy rainfall in Nashville, our hometown. The coverage was understated, and didn't indicate that we were seeing a "thousand-year flood" that would submerge parts of Nashville within two days. Some Tennessee rivers crested fourteen feet higher than their previous highs.

One television network said the storm was the worst tragedy to hit Nashville since the Civil War.

According to the National Weather Service, 18-20 inches of rain fell in some areas during two days. That more than doubled Nashville's record rainfall during Hurricane Fredrick in 1979.

The band and I went ahead and got on our flight, eager to get home. Maybe we thought we were prepared for what we might see.

But we weren't.

At perhaps three hundred feet, the length of a football field, we couldn't see familiar landmarks. They were under water. Motorboats drove in nine feet of water into the end zone at the stadium for the Tennessee Titans, our NFL football team.

The sprawling Opryland Hotel, the Grand Ole Opry House and the 94 retail stores that comprised Opry Mills resembled a giant floating ocean vessel.

Soundcheck, a storage facility that was home to hundreds of musical instruments and related equipment, resembled a building sinking into Lake Erie. The water was slowly climbing upwards.

Kurt Allison, my lead guitarist, had stored all of his recording equipment in that structure, including nine guitars, several amplifiers and other gear.

In all, $70,000 worth of his musical tools got submerged. Replacing some of those things depleted Kurt's life's savings. One of the guitars was the first he ever bought.

Instruments are to musicians what a glove is to a baseball player.

A musician has music inside of him, but releases it through his instrument. For obvious reasons, instruments are totally personal to the musicians who play them.

Kurt was understandably wounded.

Some of Kurt's belongings, including his very first guitar, were priceless. But that guitar was damaged beyond repair.

Don't get me wrong. Kurt's personal priorities were firmly in place. His loss of property meant nothing when compared to the welfare of his family and friends. All of them were fine.

I realized from Kurt and from others in the music business that *nothing* lasts forever. You can spend a lifetime collecting the tools of your trade—things that help you become the best you can be—only to see them taken away instantly.

The Nashville flood took only a few hours to change lives forever. I realized again that life is not a dress rehearsal. It's a real and one-time production.

For everyone, each day really is the first day of the rest of your life.

And I realized again that all of us are vulnerable, impressionable people.

I'm not the only person who has feelings. I'm just the person who feels my own.

Kurt's life reminded me—again—about the value of family. You may not live with them. But you can live for them.

Kurt has been with me since years before I recorded "Hicktown." He, along with Tully Kennedy and Rich Redmond, played on that record.

As I mentioned earlier in these pages, my background is similar to Tully's and Rich's, at least to some degree. It's that way with Kurt, too.

I graduated high school at age 18 and began playing in nightclubs all across the Southeast. As you know, the dates were booked by my dad.

Kurt graduated high school at age 18 and joined "Blues Other Brothers," his dad's band, a week later.

I played every weekend and many weeknights whenever my dad could schedule the shows. Kurt worked for 50 weeks during his first year with his dad.

Kurt's band traveled in vans, and slept while sitting up. So did my band and me.

I could keep on reciting my similarities with Kurt.

Realize all of that doesn't teach me a new lesson. It just confirms some of my own.

While creating music, you can invent a wonderful, unfamiliar sound while working with people from similar backgrounds. That statement is simple, but true.

I'm thankful that fate put me with musicians from simple histories. They now have colossal futures in music.

It's no secret that I love to work. In part, that's because I love the people I work with. I've known that for years.

Somewhere along the way, I realized it's hard to love anyone you don't respect. And I totally respect the genius behind each player in my band. Each guy works hard to get his sound "just right," then continues to make it even better. My players are always chasing new goals.

They love doing that, and I love their attitude. In fact, I feel the same way about my vocals.

My group and I don't "kiss up" to each other. We sometimes keep things to ourselves, but when we let loose, we tell each other the truth.

Once again, I realized the wisdom in that habit in October 2015 when I recorded a song written by Kurt, and another by Tully.

Each approached me after the session. Each said how grateful he was that I included his work on my upcoming album.

I told them both that I'd recorded his song because he'd earned it, and because it was a good song.

I meant that. And they knew it.

For a few moments, we took time and appreciated each other.

I realized how much I love what I do partly because I love the people I do it with. That's the plain truth, whether I say it too little, or sometimes not at all.

17

Benny

Singers often ask me how they can get a record deal. I cannot give them a stock answer. I don't have one. To me, there's no magic formula to ensure a business deal that will usher your recorded songs and your voice into the world.

Some people ask if self-confidence will land a deal. To that question, I actually do have a stock answer.

Believing in yourself doesn't guarantee you'll get a record deal. But failure to believe in yourself guarantees you won't.

As I've indicated previously in these pages, the only thing more powerful than believing in yourself is having someone else believe in you just as much.

In my case, I was fortunate to have several people who believed in me. They let a lot of people know about that belief, and they made sure I knew it, too.

The list includes my mom, my dad and Michael Knox.

The fourth person, someone who's maybe had the most significant impact on my career, is Benny Brown, president of Broken Bow Records, the only record company that has ever distributed my songs.

In Benny, I learned a powerful life lesson: Truly trust the people who truly trust you.

I was leery about trusting anyone in Nashville after years of knocking around Music Row and its rigid doors. People who said they were going to do certain things for my career didn't.

It was never like that with Benny and Broken Bow.

Unbeknownst to me at the time, Benny had heard a compact disc "demo" recording of my singing. It didn't blow him away. I'm not sure if that's a life lesson, but it became a career one. To this day, I'm an over-achiever regarding the perfecting of audio that will impress new fans, and retain my old ones.

Benny started BBR in 1999 from Corning, California, where he owned several automobile dealerships.

He hired a Nashville consulting service, but it often gave him bad advice. They sent him a media package about me, including demo songs and some video footage, all arranged by Kitty Moon, a woman highly respected in the music industry.

"I listened to the music," Benny said years later. "There was nothing great about it."

Benny doesn't mince words.

"Those videos sent by Kitty were what really drew me to Jason," Benny said.

He said that my stage presence on those videos drew him to me more than my singing. In fact, the videos of me performing prompted Benny to arrange a showcase for me.

Benny was wise enough to pick and choose the people who trusted him and his determination to build a successful record company.

Then one day Benny made a gesture that I'd eventually cherish. Without telling me, he came to Nashville to see me perform.

"Why hear about a person when you can see that person?" I often think to this day. That lesson applies to any kind of human relationship. Think about it.

Have you ever heard that someone can be a complete nuisance? That he or she is totally selfish? Or full of themselves? Or completely unlikeable? And then you meet them, and form your own opinion and relationship. Usually, you discover that the person isn't really public enemy number one as he or she had been portrayed by others.

Today, I don't make a complete opinion until I get the complete impression. Mine. And I make it mine based on my own decisions.

That's what Benny did regarding my music and me after he saw a video of me onstage. Later, he told me that he saw similarities among Elvis Presley, Garth Brooks and me. Can you imagine how inspired I was by someone who placed me among those household names?

Benny recalled, "I called Nashville and said, 'I'd like to see this kid'." He continued, "'But I don't want it to be a regular showcase just for music industry people. Instead, I want this showcase to be performed at the Wild Horse Saloon for the general public. And don't tell Jason that I'm coming or what I look like.'"

The show was scheduled.

I'm glad I didn't know Benny would be there. I DID NOT want to audition for another record company and a another big shot who knew nothing about my music or me. I'd done that approximately 30 times during ten years of scrambling for a record deal while living hand to mouth with my family. I'd had enough.

As I mentioned earlier, I'd once worked delivering Pepsi. On the night of Benny's showcase, my family and I had our bags packed to return to Macon, Georgia, and to Pepsi. I was scheduled to begin work in a matter of hours after my arrival.

To my dread, I had decided to do this showcase that I was sure would be my last. Why? Because when I moved my family to Macon, I was determined to leave my dreams in Nashville forever.

Little did I know that Benny's advisors did NOT agree with him about my music or me.

They didn't want Benny to schedule the showcase. They said I was old news, a familiar artist on Nashville's Music Row who had already been dropped by two labels.

Too many people in Nashville had seen me and had passed, the consultants argued. They couldn't all be wrong, Benny was told. Benny ignored their rants and listened to his instincts. He told the skeptics he was going to make me a star.

"We don't need Jason Aldean," they said. "We already have a star on BBR."

That act had recorded a number-one song but had never earned a Gold Record signifying sales of 500,000 copies.

Benny wouldn't be discouraged and said he wanted to see me perform live. That's what he wanted, and that's how it was going to be.

Had I known about all of this drama, my qualms about doing the showcase might have led to finally saying no. The last thing I needed was a bunch of "suits" telling their boss that I wasn't radio worthy, or that I'd never be successful.

But Benny kept true to his feelings and ignored theirs altogether.

Then he did something probably done for the first time ever in the history of recruiting recording talent in Nashville.

Instead of constantly looking at me on stage, he also looked squarely into the faces of people sitting beside and behind him throughout the showcase. He saw how excited they were about what they were seeing and hearing, he later told me. To this day, those people probably have no idea they were participants in Benny's personal straw poll.

And then it happened.

My years of playing in bars, of working manual jobs that I hated but always needed, my decade of searching for success I somehow couldn't find, my craving to let my music fulfill people the way it fulfilled me...all of it ended when a silver-haired, magnetic man entered slowly into the backstage room where I feared I'd just performed my final song in Nashville.

I was tired, burned out and wanted to go home where I'd sleep in Nashville for one last night.

"Hello," he said. "I'm Benny Brown."

I was going to thank him for coming, and that I'd heard about him. He didn't give me the chance.

"Welcome to Broken Bow Records," he said. "We're going to do a deal."

For a moment, I looked but didn't really see. I listened but didn't really hear.

Benny urged me to unpack my bags, and asked me not to travel back to Georgia and Pepsi in the morning.

Those were the first words of advice I remember from Benny Brown. I accepted them gratefully.

In what was minimal time for Nashville, Benny and BBR released "Hicktown," the single off my first album. The album sold 500,000 copies in twelve weeks. I received a Gold Record.

Benny knew what he was doing when he believed in me, and when he let me record "Hicktown."

In time, I gave Benny a plaque with an inscription that says: "Thanks for Making My Dreams Come True."

Through the years, I've learned things about Benny that few people know. For example, although BBR is a force in today's music industry, it isn't Benny's first dance with the music business.

Years earlier, he happened to see a 13-year-old girl singing on a country music television program in California. Her style reminded him of Patsy Cline.

Almost instantly, he believed the young lady could have a successful career, and he contacted her.

She wasn't rich, she'd never been to Nashville and she had no music business connections. Benny wanted to give her all of that and more. He believed in her that much.

He promised that he'd do his best for her with one stipulation. "Always remain the sweet and innocent person that you are now," Benny told her. "If you ever change who you are as a person, or if you ever get involved in drugs and alcohol, then I'll be done with you."

I salute Benny's courage to be direct with that young lady. His candor exhibited his personal character, I believe.

He and that adolescent girl had therefore formed a pact, and Benny kept his part of the deal. In 1987, at his own expense, Benny took the teenager to Nashville to record. Freddy Fender was then a hot act, and Benny actually arranged a duet with his unheard of vocalist and Fender.

Illness ultimately prevented the pairing, so Benny hooked her up with the legendary Faron Young. Then, back in 1990, Benny got her a record deal on Curb Records, an independent label that at one time or another had been home to Tim McGraw, Merle Haggard, LeAnn Rimes and others.

Long story short, the girl recorded a song that didn't fare well at the national level. She became disappointed and depressed, and turned to drugs and alcohol with unlikeable people.

In true form, Benny walked away from her, however rife with disappointment he was. He hasn't seen her to this day.

He kept his word. He exhibited his integrity to himself, and to the girl, who probably didn't want it. He had said what he meant, and he'd meant what he said.

Benny's brand of no-frills character remains intact to this day. It has become another of my own life's solid lessons.

# Kevin

Talent agent Kevin Neal has been one of my biggest influences for decades. He entered my life when I was sixteen years old.

Today, he oversees much of my career, just as he's done since 2004, a year before "Hicktown" became my first hit record. Kevin and I first met only two years after I'd sung those two songs at the VFW Hall in Macon, Georgia, at my public singing debut.

Then, the year I was legally allowed to drive, my dad took me to Nashville for the first time. There, he and I met with Kevin, the most effective talent booking agent at Buddy Lee Attractions (BLA), Nashville's oldest and largest privately owned talent agency.

I wasn't intimidated. In my naive youth, I didn't realize the magnitude of BLA, co-founded in 1964 by Hank Williams' wife, Audrey Williams, after Hank died in 1953.

In time, Buddy Lee Attractions would represent the biggest country stars of all-time, including Garth Brooks, Willie Nelson and George Strait.

Yet, in 1993, my dad fearlessly introduced me to Kevin who'd one day become president of BLA.

So there I was, barely old enough to shave, with my dad who wouldn't be discharged from the Air Force for two more years.

How could Dad and I possibly tap the interest of Kevin? Garth was on top of the entertainment world. Strait was accumulating number-one songs, which would one-day total 66. Willie, the legendary singer/songwriter, was a national hero for having earlier founded Farm Aid to assist distressed family farms.

And I was just a "wannabe" from Macon. I couldn't even legally enter bars. (So I continued to sneak inside to play them.)

I'd also never heard of the William Morris Agency, THE biggest talent and management agency in all of show business representing singers, dancers, actors, directors, producers, authors and more. I had no idea that William Morris would eventually open a Nashville office, merge with Endeavor Talent Agency, and become an even larger agency!

Kevin would leave BLA to become a full fledged partner in William Morris Endeavor (WME) in 2015.

But on the day I first met Kevin, he focused on this country boy and his dad standing beside him. How many big shots would have done that?

When asked why Kevin had taken the time to see me, he said an old friend of his, Joe Lennane, and my dad had asked him to. That was it. This career builder met "Jason Unheard Of" simply because he'd been asked by Joe.

"Everything happens for a reason," Kevin told me during our first encounter . . . "*everything*."

Time and time again, I'd hear Kevin repeat those words before I officially became a BLA client and before I released a major recording. His loyalty to me was similar to that of my parents, and eventually Michael Knox and my band members.

The value of Kevin's trustworthiness would one day teach me a simple but important lesson:

"Be loyal to people who are loyal to you."

In show business, I've amassed untold hundreds of "friends." But many are "artificial friends." Those supposed friends are merely glorified acquaintances. I think most everyone has friends like that.

Personally, I define friendship as lasting and enduring. As I've indicated, some of my best friends are my biological family members. They stick with me whether I'm up or down or in between. When they know I'm falling, they catch me. When they think I'm rising, they cheer me on.

Our minds and emotions don't always agree. But neither ever wears out. Their staying power is fueled by loyalty and love.

Similarly, through Kevin, I realized that, whether or not members are blood relatives, families are sometimes formed around a common cause. A part of my family is therefore made up of people who are as passionate about music as I am.

Through Kevin, I also realized once again that career families often fight with words as their weapons. Their closeness to each other allows them to say what they feel, and feel what they say, and even get sad or angry or hurt. But when the clashes are over, the grudges dissolve. Then the professional family resumes their mutual objectives.

Kevin recently remembered two incidents when I was angry with him. Both became nothing more than bumps on the road in our careers and our relationship.

The first happened when Kevin scheduled the band and me for two 90-minute back-to-back shows at a West Virginia fair. In the heat of summer, we played on a stage without a roof. It was hot!

The band and I kinda staggered off the platform headed for our air-conditioned bus. But the concert promoter had other ideas.

He wanted the musicians and me to do a "meet and greet," a mixer with fans to sign autographs and take photographs.

I'm usually happy to do that, but only when I can do it at my best. I appreciate my fans, on or off the stage. But on this particular date, exhaustion told me I couldn't give my fans my best.

The promoter was furious, the fans were disappointed and I blamed Kevin.

We laugh about it today.

My second outburst toward Kevin involved George Strait, someone I'd never met when my fury transpired. Strait was one of my musical mentors. I sang his songs on stage well before and long after I got my record deal. Strait has never had a bigger fan than me.

I had often told Kevin, an amateur photographer, to photograph Strait and me should our paths ever cross.

As fate would have it, I played a music festival with Strait and others. Afterwards, thanks to arrangements made by Kevin, I walked to Strait's bus and stood by the door.

Out came Strait with Norma, his wife, and Erv Woolsey, his manager. I was with Kevin.

The five of us talked for half an hour, maybe longer. Kevin had his camera.

"Let's see the pictures you took of George and me!" I excitedly asked afterwards.

Kevin hadn't taken any. Lost in the moment, he'd completely forgotten!!

My meeting Strait was like a young golfer meeting Tiger Woods. But the pictures of our meeting were lodged only in my memory. I was really steamed at Kevin for days.

But I never thought about leaving him, especially for anything that trite. Loyal friends don't leave. Besides, without Kevin, I wouldn't have been booked on that show.

Kevin recently recalled another incident that stirred my feelings toward my non-blood-related beloved family members.

It seems I'd told people in my entourage what most already knew—that I consider all of them surrogate family. I want fans and associates to treat my stagehands the same way they treat me. I want identical treatment toward my sound guys, my bus drivers, my merchandise sellers...anyone who's a part of my show who pours out energy and heart, only to pack up and race hundreds of miles to do it all again.

A former road manager didn't agree. He said that I felt like I was the star of my show with no regard to other people in my organization. I knew better, and so did my people.

That road manager apparently didn't think we were a traveling family. He apparently thought everyone was concerned only for himself or herself.

If he believed we're all loners, he'd also feel comfortable while alone.

So I fired him. Then, like a lesson I'd learned from Kevin, I let his memory dissolve.

# 19

# Trust

**P**eople usually like people before they trust them. People must also understand people before they trust them. I realized that as I watched Kevin Neal follow my struggling and early career.

In those days, to understand me was to understand my music. Kevin learned that my music and I were often one and the same.

I learned that by watching him as he listened to me at those failed showcases.

He attended most of them during the 1990s and early 2000s when I was chasing a record deal. He was paid nothing.

Earlier in these pages, I mentioned my strong belief in the power of persistence. Kevin confirmed it. He always believed I'd get a recording contract, eventually. Sometimes, he believed it more than I did.

"Jason contacted me and said he was going to do show-cases," Kevin recently recalled. "I started going to his showcases to see who he was. I'm sure I went to a dozen or more."

Who does that? Only someone who truly believes in you.

I'm not green. I know that Kevin also came on behalf of his own career. He wanted to represent me for personal engagements once I finally got a record deal.

All the while, my Nashville showcases became kinda routine and routinely disappointing.

The band and I would knock out the audience. They'd dance, sing and applaud wildly. Meanwhile, the record company big shots sat stiffly. Then they'd leave the show and I'd never hear from them.

"I saw the big picture in Jason," Kevin said years later. "I didn't understand why the record people weren't getting it. He was frustrated and so was I."

By his own words, Kevin was baffled. But he stayed in my creative corner. In a nutshell, he persisted in trusting in me just as I trusted in him.

He was in the audience that night when I was preparing to move back to Macon, Georgia, after seven years of fighting and failing within the Nashville system. While I was singing, he was telling Broken Bow Records' executives they should sign me to their label. His mere presence as Buddy Lee Attractions' foremost booking agent was a powerful endorsement in my behalf.

Once my signing with BBR was finalized, I needed a booking agent. Without hesitation, I went instantly to Kevin.

The unpaid guy who'd attended my unpaid showcases today oversees the scheduling of all of my performances. During ten years at BBR and the sales of more than 34 million downloaded songs, I've consistently seen Kevin help direct my career growth while growing in our friendship.

We became the fulfillment of my life's lesson. That is, we liked each other, and did so before we grew to trust each other.

After I had a record deal, I waited for a long time before receiving any income. During those months, I hadn't even released my first single. Concert promoters across America hadn't heard of me so they obviously hadn't heard my music. Why would they pay significant money to hear my band and me perform?

Most wouldn't.

Once again, Kevin asked me to trust him, and insisted he knew what he was doing when asking me to play shows for little money or none at all. Trust him I did—again.

"It's not about making money," Kevin continued. "It's about grinding it out and playing markets that are going to help you in the future."

"Okay, let's do it," I'd said.

"It was wonderful to have Jason's blind faith in me," Kevin recalled. "Jason was saying, 'you've been doing this for a long time, so whatever you say, I'll trust you so let's go do this!'"

And Kevin proved to be correct.

I had faith in him because I'd previously seen his faith in me when few other people did.

Meanwhile, I didn't know that Kevin was calling in favors from nightclub owners and concert promoters who'd previously bought his other acts. He assured each that I would soon have a song on the radio. He took it a step farther, and said I'd become a "big star."

I wouldn't have said that about me. I'd have waited to see what time presented.

But Kevin told those buyers they should book me at their venues, and do it while I was affordable.

Perhaps he told some that if they'd book me now, they could have me at a discount when my records begin climbing the charts. Whatever Kevin did, it worked. Those show promoters again trusted him, just as I did.

So, the less-than-famous tour headlined by an unknown singer and his band began.

We played Bristol, Tennessee, for $500.00. There was little profit for us after we bought bus fuel, motel rooms and food. But Bristol's leading disc jockey came to our show. After seeing it, he promised to play my first record on BBR, no matter what the song. That scene played out over and over across the nation.

Kevin asked me to play Charlotte, North Carolina, three times in twelve months! I thought that was overexposure. But, once again, I trusted Kevin for his career experiences, and for his confidence in me.

"You're not trying to get rich," he often insisted. "That will come later. You're instead building a fan base. When your first record comes out, those fans will know you. Then, they'll buy it, and they'll tell their friends to do the same thing."

So we pressed on as musicians who sometimes worked for less money than we'd earned before we had a record deal! Time would tell that Kevin knew exactly what he was doing.

In October 2004, he booked the band and me into a nightclub in Lakeland, Florida. Before we arrived, a hurricane had knocked out the nightclub's windows and permanent sound system!

Kevin told us to play the date anyway. He said the owner had placed audio speakers onto sticks that held them upright.

Once we arrived, we had no rooms. Motels had been damaged or destroyed. The remaining were filled with storm victims.

Due to high water, the band and I couldn't even drive the bus to a YMCA. Instead, we rolled our baggage to it just to take showers.

We entered the giant club where fewer than fifty people had weathered the storm to come to our show.

Kevin told us to do what we would have done anyway—to play as if we were in a giant stadium. And we did.

A year later, I was doing my album release tour. The band and I played that same club. It was filled to capacity and many fans were turned away.

They wanted to see me because those 50 people had told their friends about our show, and how we now had a major record album.

Kevin had been correct. When done right, professional exposure will grow.

When done right, so will personal trust.

# 20

# Justin

Justin Weaver and I have been friends since we were 16, back when he led a house band at a nightclub. I asked to sing two or three songs with the group, and wound up becoming a regular guest artist.

That band played five grueling hours nightly with only three 15-minute breaks. During that time, Justin sat under a light in the back of the bar where he did his homework. (One day, he'd become a guitarist in the Young Guns.)

Justin's unusual study habits were one of my first lessons about focus. He sat solidly and did his homework while the band was blaring and people were dancing and yelling. He loved live music, but temporarily forced himself to ignore it. Instead, he kept on adding, multiplying, dividing and subtracting numbers to fulfill his next day's school assignment.

"Who could do that in this environment?" I thought. "Who'd want to ignore the party while sitting in the middle of it?"

Justin sometimes asked me to sing longer just so he'd have more time for homework.

Not exactly a school junkie myself, I hadn't yet realized that Justin could multi-task many things if they tapped into his passions. Justin's obsession was to become a successful songwriter.

To this day, I love to work with people who are a part of my history. I've learned that a "comfort zone" surrounds those pairings. I've also learned that original ideas spring from familiar minds. They have compatible, creative chemistry.

That's exactly what happened in 2004 when Justin and I wrote "Even If I Wanted To." We penned that song on a Friday. I recorded it the following Tuesday for my first album.

We made the creative process look easy. But it was anything but. Many years of emotionally draining days and nights preceded that three-minute song.

You've read about some of my own challenges in previous pages. But from the time Justin and I were teenagers, I've learned from him.

At age 14, he and his dad came to Nashville where neither knew anyone, not one person. After graduating from Georgia College & State University, Justin returned with his wife, Heather. They lived with me for two weeks.

As a guide for job leads, Justin's dad had given him the names of several music publishing companies. Trouble is, his dad didn't know those publishers himself.

He'd simply torn out all music publisher listings from Nashville's telephone directory's Yellow Pages.

Justin began a songwriting career while armed only with those faded pages and his knuckles. He used his knuckles to knock on doors. Over the course of 66 knocks on 66 doors, Justin was always turned away. Or sometimes, his songs were actually heard before he was told his material was unwanted.

Imagine that much rejection. Imagine how many times Justin wondered if moving his family to Nashville from Georgia to pursue his dreams was founded in bravery or foolishness. But he stayed.

And he knocked. And knocked.

During those stressful days, Justin's wife worked as a first grade schoolteacher and he freelanced as a copyeditor.

As Justin's songs were continually rejected, he continued to write new ones. He simply refused to give in to a business that continued to reject him. Perhaps you could say that he was driven by fear of failure. Failure, after all, is guaranteed only if you quit.

But with so much failure Justin eventually suffered an emotional meltdown.

"At that point," Justin thought, "I'm searched out. I don't know what else to do or where to go. And I'd only been to about thirty music publishers. So I begged the guy."

"'Dude,'" I said, "'I will do coffee, I will wash dishes, I will stay after writing sessions, I will vacuum floors, I'll do extra work if y'all can get me on payroll.' I heard my voice cracking."

"I didn't realize how desperate I'd sounded until after the fact," Justin recalled. "When I left that office, I was appalled and disgusted at myself. And he didn't give me a job . . . of course not."

After nine months, on his sixty-seventh attempt, Justin landed his first publishing deal. He had fought the good fight, and he'd won!

I was reminded again what I'd often learned from Justin's and others' accomplishments, including my own. Once you achieve a goal, you forget your old struggles. Then you inherit new ones.

Justin and I once argued about a song he wrote. He didn't want me to put a "hold" on it, or reserve the tune, until I was going to record an album nine months later. He instead wanted to pitch the song to Tim McGraw who was scheduled to record in three weeks.

But I made some calls and got a "hold" on the song. That meant no one could record that tune except me for an allotted amount of time. It never became hit. Later, Justin wished he'd gotten it to Tim. He still reminds me about that.

Justin and I once got into an argument in a recording studio control booth where he hit me in the face. He insisted that punch was an accident. I disagreed.

Our voices were raised and we began pushing each other. The studio owner was overwhelmed, and shoved Justin and me into the hallway. He feared our clash would become a full-blown brawl, and that we'd crash into his expensive electronic equipment. He was really mad.

That ordeal reminded me of something I'd learned years earlier.

When you and a friend can be honest enough to speak your minds, and those words prompt a fight, then you later forget about it, well, you know you've got a real friend, not someone who pretends to be a friend just because he wants to make money off of you.

Justin's and my friendship rises above some Nashville phonies and their gold digging.

I've also learned something else from a few people, including Justin, about genuine friendship. You know you have a real friend when he's truly happy for your success, and you're truly happy for his.

Justin validated that theory once again when I found myself thrilled over his highly successful songs. To date, he's written over 100 songs that have been recorded.

He got a "cut" (a song) on "Title," Meghan Trainor's first album, the one that included "It's All About That Bass," a song that has sold more than 11 million copies worldwide.

Justin wrote "Like I'm Gonna Lose You," a hit single by Meghan and John Legend.

Justin had a song recorded by Brantley Gilbert and it became his first number-one hit!

Realize that Justin is a man's man. But at a party to celebrate his first number-one song, he cried.

I totally understood.

And once again, I knew that every action, no matter how simple, will always prompt a reaction, even if it's simply sitting in with someone's band so he can do his homework.

# Compromise

I've loved deer hunting all of my life. As a boy, I shared those wonderful times with Arthur Aldine Williams, my grandfather, who died when I was fourteen.

After that, I stayed out of the woods for a while. I thought about earlier hunting trips, and wondered what future trips would be like without him.

Eventually, I returned to the woods with a crossbow, camouflaged clothes, the natural scents of crisp fall mornings and all the rest for a hunter searching for a good time. And maybe, I just might kill a buck. Whether or not I got a deer, I was always pleased whenever I was in the woods.

Earlier in these pages, I talked about growing up and playing sports and going to school and riding in a Pepsi truck and struggling in Nashville and getting a record deal and having hit songs and giant concerts. All of that slowly changed my life and my priorities.

But my love of hunting has stayed with me through all of those years, although there were times, due to financial stress or being busy, when I couldn't hunt as much as I do today.

A few years ago, my life as a hunter reached a major peak when some guys called me after starting "Buck Commander," a television reality show about deer hunting. They asked me to go hunting with them! Eventually, I became a co-owner of the show, and appeared in episodes with other hunters, including Willie Robertson, Ryan Langerhans, Adam LaRoche, Luke Bryan and Tombo Martin.

That show got into my blood. To me, hunting rose to a higher level when a cameraman was shooting my every move, along with the sly maneuvers of a deer. After a day of hunting, the camera also made relaxing around the campfire extra fun. That happy-go-lucky atmosphere, including fresh meat and beer, made life just about as good as it can get.

On one episode, Adam gave a lesson about deer hunting skills. Willie must not have been interested. He kept dozing off—on national television! Who couldn't avoid laughing at that?

Another time, one of our buddies visited our camp in a worn-out junk heap of a car. As the night got later, the laughter got louder about that ugly vehicle. A bulldozer happened to be nearby, so I drove it over the car, smashing it into a steel pancake. The next day, the driver had to return the junker on a flatbed truck.

He told the rental people that he'd bought the twenty-five dollar insurance policy, and hoped it covered flattened cars!

Still another time, someone put a rat in Luke's backpack. When he reached inside, he yelled and nearly jumped out of his skin, but not before the rat bit off a tiny part of his finger.

"Buck Commander" is good-ole-boy, Southern humor. People who hunt and people who don't both seem to like it.

It's similar to "Duck Dynasty," a reality show where Willie is a cast member. That format must be working, too. The show has been around for almost a decade.

Willie officiated the ceremony marrying me to the former Brittany Kerr, a beautiful woman who has never watched "Buck Commander."

Now, as Brittany and I are approaching our fourth year together, she still hasn't seen the show, even though we shoot it at scenic places, and the production is funny one minute and suspenseful the next. Brittany would enjoy all of that—if it weren't for one thing.

A show about deer hunting sometimes shows deer getting killed.

"I get nervous," she said. "I'm afraid I'll see something that will get me upset, so I just don't watch 'Buck Commander.'"

That's the reason I go hunting and the reason she won't. I'm an animal hunter married to an animal rights enthusiast.

"When he's on a hunt, I stay at home," she said. "And if he goes hunting, I don't want to know anything about it. So when he comes home, I don't ask any questions. I hope he's safe, then I let him go about his day."

I remember my early years when hunting was the pastime that eventually became my passion. Brittany remembers her childhood critters, including frogs, lizards and snakes. She even had a python as a pet! How many girls do that?

Once, I walked out of our house in my hunting clothes and she cried.

"What's wrong?" I asked her. "You knew that I was going hunting."

"I know," she said, "But seeing you like that makes it worse."

And so it goes. I can stand in front of 100,000 fans and make them happy. I can dress in camouflage and stand in front of my wife and make her miserable.

These days, I don't put on my hunting clothes until after I'm gone. I don't talk about hunting, and she doesn't talk about it either. Meanwhile, Brittany and I have something else in common.

Love.

Love is a give and take situation. When I don't talk about hunting, I don't see that as a compromise. I instead see it as another way I can show my love for Brittany, the woman who introduced me to real love after all.

Brittany also sees compromise as a blessing. We simply love to love each other.

That's how we make this marriage work.

More than ever, Brittany and I have learned something else about love. It's contagious.

Not long after she and I began dating, Brittany and I visited Debbie Wood, my birth mother. My mom and I then introduced

Brittany to Kendyl and Keeley, my daughters, who are now ages ten and fourteen.

I hoped the girls would like Brittany, and soon thereafter, they fell in love with her. That's another thing about love. People can see it, and I was no exception.

In a short time, Keeley and Brittany realized they have "girly" interests in common, such as clothes and makeup. Kendyl loves animals, which made her instantly compatible with Brittany for obvious reasons.

Today, the girls visit with Brittany and me every other weekend, and sometimes more. Often, the three of them get their nails manicured, and I'm not a part of that. But mostly, we four have fun by going to movies or to a "Jungle Gym" or just staying at home and watching television or playing video games.

Our favorite television show is "Impractical Jokers," and we've almost mastered "Mario Kart," our favorite video game.

Going out with my daughters is the only time I refuse to take photographs with fans. When I'm with my girls it's "their" time when memories are made.

Kendyl and Keeley are my life's brightest lights, those that help me to see through the dark times, the likes of which everyone faces in life.

Just as Brittany fills the role of my wife, my girls fulfill my yearning for father-daughter companionship.

Sometimes, just the sight of my wife and two daughters make me feel sorry.

Sorry, that is, for anyone who doesn't happen to be me.

# Epilogue

I sometimes think about the people who founded the country music industry, and realize they had no idea that the music would one day be the nation's most popular and that Nashville would become one of the highest-profiled cities in the United States.

Through all of this runaway success and municipal growth, I have realized that the country music industry is setting new popularity statistics every month. But who comprises the industry?

People, that's who.

I'm blessed to live and work in Nashville where I'm a player in this unprecedented growth and popularity of the music I grew up singing, whether in my house, a car or on a barroom stage. Of course, the music has changed a lot since then.

Change is the stimulant for growth. If something doesn't grow, it dies. People who resent change and growth should realize that both are better than death.

Today, I'm a guy who's learned many lessons, including lessons about lessons—really.

My life's lessons have a spirit of their own, and are often spontaneous. They often burst into my mind from wherever and whenever they want. They occasionally evolve from unexpected circumstances and unexpected people. Other times, they arrive by invading my thoughts when I'm alone and thinking because there's nothing else to do. And I'm sometimes surprised by the end result.

For example, as a child I had no idea that my dad's singing and playing music would plant the desire in me to do the same. I had no idea that singing inside our little house or playing in the yard would launch my yearning to sing for others that eventually would become masses.

Big things are sometimes birthed by little ones, or so I've learned.

I had no idea that my simply giving my approval for my sister to date my best friend would evolve into their marriage and parenthood. I therefore learned that granting a wish to determined people can evolve into something wonderful.

I've learned that no matter how much I love someone, I can love them more.

I've learned to listen when a lot of people say the same thing. Usually, that many people can't be wrong, but that doesn't always mean they're right.

I'm someone who's defined, in part, by his career. My work doesn't come with a guaranteed Friday paycheck, or a 401K or a pension. It's not just a job. It's an investment in myself.

The more I pour of myself into my livelihood, the more it rewards me.

I've also learned that I can't control many of life's circumstances. But I can control how I'll react to them.

Show business is an uncertain environment with a few underhanded people. Virtually all of the singers I know have a few hair-raising stories about abuses from their promoters, managers, booking agents or other performers.

For some of those artists, the injustices were too much, and they drowned in their pool of self-pity. They hit bottom, and decided they liked it there, as it offered no risks or cruelty. It also offered no progress or fulfillment.

A lot of that made me realize that life isn't fair, but it's better than the alternative. And there's always another day, and another chance to change things, or to be changed.

I hope that some of my life's lessons shared in this book will prompt favorable lessons for you too. If so, my mission is accomplished, and my life will continue, in some part, as a continuous song.

Through the pages of this book, I hope you feel as though you've gotten to know me, at least to a degree. And even if we never sing side by side, we will have somehow sung together.

# About the Authors

Jason Aldean, the two-time Academy of Country Music's "Entertainer of the Year," has sold more than 16 million albums and has nineteen #1 songs. He has been the ACM's "Male Vocalist of the Year" three times. The sale of his downloads surpasses those of any other male artist in country music history. He is a standing-room-only attraction at NFL and NBA stadiums and arenas, and fills major league baseball parks, among other venues. He lives with his wife, Brittany, outside of Nashville, Tennessee. He has two daughters, Kendyl and Keeley.

Tom Carter has written 19 books, nine of which were *New York Times* or *USA Today* best-sellers. He has collaborated to write books with Reba McEntire, Britney Spears, Glen Campbell, Merle Haggard, George Jones, Ronnie Milsap and many others. He lives with his wife, Janie, in Nashville, Tennessee.

CPSIA information can be obtained
at www.ICGtesting.com
Printed in the USA
LVHW01*0855271017
553872LV00002B/12/P